C000137267

TERENCE HORSLEY

FISHING
AND
FLYING

TERENCE HORSLEY

FISHING
AND
FLYING

ILLUSTRATIONS BY
C.F. TUNNICLIFFE

UNICORN

Published in 2016 by Unicorn,
an imprint of Unicorn Publishing Group
101 Wardour Street
London
W1F 0UG
www.unicornpress.org

Image © C. F. Tunnicliffe
Text © Terence Horsley

ISBN 978-1-910787-13-7

5 4 3 2 1

First published in 1947

All rights reserved. No part of this publication may be reproduced in
any form or by any means without permission of the publishers.

The publisher has made every effort to contact the current copyright
holders. Any commission is unintentional and the publisher would be
pleased to hear from any copyright holder not acknowledged.

Designed by Anna Hopwood
Printed in Spain by GraphyCems

• CONTENTS •

to

THE GIRL I LEFT
BEHIND

I

Flying

F rom fifteen thousand feet above the wildest, the most precipitous, and the loneliest part of the highlands, the land below looks flat and innocuous. I have lingered in the sunlight above the peaks of the Cairngorms, and marveled at the apparent innocence of the land. It lies below like an open book, without mystery, or even particular charm, varying only in colour. The darker shades predominate, purple-greys in pools merging into russets, which in turn bleach into the lighter shades of ochre. Among these shapes are winding arms of sombre green which twist towards the edges of the horizon, each one vitalised by a silver vein. Here and there a swollen pool of this life blood lies serene among the rhomboids of the flat board. This is Scotland, this is the terrain of the deer forests and the great rivers, the lochs, the precipices, the peat bogs, and the open wastes of moor.

It is unconvincing until some whimsy prompts you to take another view. There was a day when I did this, throwing away not only the prospect I have described, but its frame as well a frame made of the sea glint in the north by the Moray Firth and its eastward sweep to where the land ends at Rattray Head, and south again past Aberdeen, and nearly down to the Forth, and then west across the blue-grey mountains to the silver gleam of the Atlantic a prospect which was impressive in its geography if only because of its extent.

I threw it away in a dive, swallowing and shouting on the way down to relieve the mounting pressure on the ear drums, so that in less time than it would have taken to cross a London street I was carried into the womb of the mountains, to be enclosed and overshadowed. I hurtled down the Larrig Ghru at two hundred feet that desolate gap in the hills whose winter snows claim their victims every year shooting between the four thousand foot peaks of Ben Macdhui and Braeriach, to skim the gushing burn which, in a few minutes, became the river Dee. It was perhaps ten miles in distance through the Larrig, but in time it was a breath, and almost immediately I was swinging up again in a broad turn to do battle with the peaks. Here was Loch Einich which I had last seen through a blizzard when I had made an attempt to climb the four peaks in a single day.

The rock cliffs which spring from its shore flashed past the wing tip and swept to a serrated parapet. Even with two thousand horses at my command I felt small and powerless beside them. Another sweep carried me along the forest edges which mark the valley of the Spey, before I climbed again into the hills. This time I flicked across the bowl which holds the loneliest and the highest loch in Scotland, the granite saucer carved in the shoulder of Cairn Toule. When I was here before, the snow cornices overhung the saucer's edge, unclimbable, frozen, with a beard of white whipped from its rim by the wind. Today the rocks were black, cleaned of snow by a summer which for once had lingered. And yet as I sped down the slopes at three hundred miles an hour the devil of fear which seemed to lurk on these heights had his hand on my shoulder. What if my horses should fail? There wasn't a level place to land for miles. A friend who had survived such a landing had walked for seventeen hours before he came to a house. I had to look up and feel the friendly warmth of the sun to be reassured.

I picked up the young Dee where the tree line reaches the skirts of the Cairngorms, and flying east followed it into Balmoral Forest. But on either side the hills were split by the glens, and one of them leading to the south attracted me. I flew in low, and the brow of Lochnagar overhung the instruments as I skirted its twisting flanks. In a moment it was necessary to lift the plane over an outlying shoulder, to drop down beyond to the deserted waters of Loch Muick.

Now once again I was lost in a waste of heather, bog, and wicked peaks. Southwards at four miles to every minute I flew among their nodding heads, until the ground split and the headwaters of the

South Esk were suddenly below. I found myself looking down a tunnel of cliffs which ran for ten miles to Milton of Clava, a place where I had been to watch the salmon spawn. In the year when the snow lay so heavily in the glen (1941 I think it was) a misguided explorer had flown in from the opposite direction, and found that he neither had the power to climb fast enough to get out, or sufficient room to turn round. So he flew on, until he settled like a fly on the face of the mountain.

In a matter of a few minutes I had visited three great rivers, the Spey flowing north, and the Dee and the South Esk, flowing east and separated by forty miles on the coast.

Now I turned south west and flew across the run of the valleys on the east side of the Grampians. It is well loved country, birth place of some happy memories, and some others which, in retrospect at least, were happy. It wasn't more than a couple of minutes after leaving the South Esk before I was over the headwaters of the Isla, switch backing down the carries. Here was a deer forest, as naked as the day when primitive man, like his successors, decided it was no place for his habitation. There are grander peaks than Monameanach, and Mayar. Indeed, Mayar is only three thousand feet high. Yet whether you flash down their sides in an aeroplane, or trudge with seeming unending rhythm on your feet, they impress you with nobility, remoteness, and even with fear. I paused for a moment, flinging the aircraft into a tight circle while gravity thrust me down into the seat until the sky went grey. In the narrow compass which I described I spent a whole day stalking a hind. In a few seconds I had made my circuit. To have walked it even on this lovely summer afternoon would have taken hours, while on that bitter day the previous winter I had walked from dawn to dusk.

I have known literate people who think of a deer forest as a wooded paradise where the mountains are a picturesque background. The truth is, perhaps, that they have never left the roads to penetrate deep enough through the twisting valleys, till the rivers become streams, and the streams burns, and the burns trickles, till the last sign of a house or a tree is a memory hours old.

I straightened the aircraft and pulled her into a sensational climb. In a moment there were two thousand feet between the mountains and I. They looked small and innocent again, and over their intervening crests I found myself looking down into the main valley, seeing the dark blur of the lowland woods, and here and there the roof of a croft. The deer forest melted into the background as I sped southwards, devouring the glens in a spate of speed and leaving whole worlds behind where highlanders have lived out the span of their lives. This flying at once achieves the miraculous, but in doing so it misses the common standards by which mortals live.

So I continued south and had glimpse of the Tay Estuary thirty miles out over the port wing tip, the city of Dundee a dark smudge on its banks. For a moment I dived low over Loch Lintrathen, over its west bay where I had hooked a two pound trout and poached a Mallard with a rifle. Twenty miles on I crossed the gap in the mountains furrowed by the Tay above Perth, and here I turned north, flew low again, and made the hills echo with the rude voice of the engine. I left the Tay and devoured the gorge of the Tummel, to sweep over the bridge where on a fine summer day I had lured a salmon with a trout fly, hooked it, and finally lost it all for the price of a trout fisher's licence. The tourist agencies send their fleets of buses this way, and the thought sickened me as my own rude advent must have sickened those highland folk whose lives even then I was so wantonly disturbing. The stalker, the fisherman, the shooter, and the climber are the legitimate visitors to the fastnesses over which I was flying, and in the air the sky belongs to the eagle. Low flying aeroplanes are an offence, and in retrospect I feel penitent for what I did that day. It is incongruous enough to see the brightly coloured buses crawling along the twisting glens, and to follow in their wake of discarded offal. They in their good time will destroy the spirit of the mountains. The electrification schemes with their plans for industry will set their seal upon the work, so that we shall see the glens barricaded with mighty walls of concrete and the pleasant lowlands teeming with profitable industry. It would be a poor thing if I myself on this lovely day were to be regarded as a forerunner of the aerial hordes. Happily the breath of the hills will make such a thing unlikely, for I doubt whether there is one day in thirty when such a ride as I was taking would be tolerable. Around the shoulders of the mountains the wind gushes in uncertain eddies, and over their crests it boils, invisible, but with a fury which will throw an aircraft for scores of feet in any direction. Only in conditions of a deep anti-cyclonic calm might one expect the smooth air I was enjoying.

I steered for the mountains to the north west, skimming the roofs of Pitlochry, where the hotel gave the impression of mammoths escaped from a zoo, north west around Ben Vrackie looking like a boulder left after the gods had been at play, north west into the un-peopled wastes of Glen Garry where only the railway and the thin road beside it make a pretence of man's sovereignty. And so it was that I came again into the valley of the Spey, this time at its headwaters facing the Monadhliath Mountains. I had made the round, a circuit adapted for a month's walking tour, a week's motoring, or better still, a lifetime for living. I had been flying for forty five minutes, and because in the factual world from which I had come I was engaged on a routine test of one of His Majesty's fighters, I considered it was time that I returned. So over the headwaters of the Spey, which I have never fished and always longed to do, I again pointed my aircraft at the sky and once more made Scotland shrink into a flat chequerboard of haphazard patterns. In another quarter of an hour I was riding down the eastern slopes of the hills, opening up the sea coast and the lesser range of the Sidlaws, lower and lower until the green fields sped beneath and it was time to lower the undercarriage.

And what profit is there that man shall consume the beauties of the earth in such gulps? It is a difficult question, for it implies theneed for an answer to the relative merits of two, twenty, and two hundred miles an hour. Were we living in the age of the horse there could never be any such question. But speed is a substance of unstable qualities, varying from generation to generation as widely as politics. Certain it is that the places we love were once never far from the places where we lived, and that a jog trot was well suited to the times. It would perhaps have meant that if I had lived two hundred years ago I should never have seen the highlands. But then I should never have seen much else which detracts from the pleasure of living in the coal yard, for instance, above which many of these words were written, nor the electric railway, nor the dome of the Albert Hall which rises above the chimney pots like the amputated breast of a corpse. Nor should I have breathed the dry, centrally heated air of a room which was scarcely the size of a dog kennel, or listened to the crisp whine of rubber tyres on the roadway below, or to other people's wireless sets playing in adjoining flats, or to the whir of the electric lift outside the door. Two hundred years lies a long way down the tunnel of time, and maybe we see the past at the end of it as something more desirable than it really was. But however true that may be, the call of the earth which lies over the boundaries of the modern industrial belts is a clear call. Even from the sixth floor of a London block of flats I could sometimes see the sun, and being human felt myself permitted to wonder what was happening beyond my smoky horizons. It is at times like these that the less desirable qualities of the aeroplane lose their sting. The noise of the engine fades, its disturbance to others seems unimportant, and all that is left is the thought that in an hour, perhaps two hours, the places we love can be reached. For me the air has been a means to an end, and is so wrapped up in all that I have enjoyed that it has become entangled with what I write.

Give a man an aeroplane, a fishing rod, a scatter gun and a rifle, and he can still break out of the crowds. At two hundred miles an hour, Cornwall is a little over sixty minutes from Heston, while those peaks of the Cairngorms from which I looked down are hardly two hours away. A page from an old diary lends colour to the idea.

'This morning I escaped from London again. It was a grey day back there, and as the electric train carried me out to the aerodrome I doubted whether I should be able to take off. In the 'Met' office they told me that a front was sweeping up the channel from the south west, but if I hurried I should be ahead of it and would draw out into clear weather. And hurry I did, for London these days has few attractions. In an hour I saw the towers of York Cathedral, in two hours I was across the Firth of

Forth, and in less than three I was kicking into life the engine of 'Old Faithful' (the motor cycle which was garaged in Scotland against such expeditions as these).

'Angus had the boat waiting for me as I knew he would after receiving my postcard. I had bent the trees round his house with the blast of my propeller as I had flown in and he had come out and waved.

'Now I am drifting along the south side of the island, casting the old favourites on the rippling water. Slim chance I have, for the light is brilliant, the whole sky aflame as the sun sets. Yet in the sound of the ripple against the planking of the boat, soft as a mother's lullaby, there is a great peace. It seems impossible that only a few hours ago I was one of seven million others in crowded London.'

I must admit that in the winter an aeroplane is a less certain method of travel than a train or a motor car. But as a wartime pilot, air travel was the order of the day and one acquired a degree of cunning at getting through bad weather, which at less urgent moments might have suggested a sleeping berth on a train. But what with the lack of trains and the almost complete disappearance of their sleeping berths a risk or two in an aeroplane was preferable. Like most other pilots, I believed it better to die sitting down in a well-designed cockpit than to be crushed to death on my feet in the corridor of an express. The risk at any rate was soon over, for at the speeds attainable by the faster types of service aircraft a journey from one end of the land to the other was completed before the weather had time to change its mind. And even if the worst came to the worst, there was usually a diligent person at the stationary end of a radio telephone anxious to give a pilot who mixed up, say the Manchester fog with the Sheffield smoke blackout, his bearings.

Conditions may be different in the future. They are beginning to be different even now. Those of us who were in the flying services do not expect to go on burning up the countryside at speeds of four hundred miles an hour, with petrol consumptions in the region of a hundred gallons an hour – at least not at the expense of the taxpayer. Private flyers are entering a more leisurely age, whatever the prophets say to the contrary. Not that we are being driven out of the air: we are merely cutting our cloth with regard to our purses. My own prospective cloth is of a quiet pattern and envisages a cabin monoplane of a mere hundred horse power and a speed of less than two miles a minute. These are low figures by the standards popularly associated with modern aircraft. But they remain close to the best that is obtainable in conjunction with economy.

Those who accept the chance to fly in the years to come will be less regretful of its lack of power or of its ultimate speed than they will be impressed by the new conception they will gain of familiar places. In the novelty of seeing the world afresh, they will forget to yearn for the speeds which are born only of many hundreds of horse power crammed into a small, and by comparison uncomfortable, aircraft. The vision of their land seen from above will be responsible for a great mental change of outlook, so that not only will their sense of distance be readjusted, but their ideas of what does, in fact, constitute their land will be changed. They will be seeing the country for the first time in terms of its colours. Were I to be blindfolded and to be flown anywhere in England or Scotland, I believe that I could pin-point myself by the shades of the ground and the pattern of the agriculture below. Not only are the white cliffs of Dover and the red earth of Devon equally effective signs from the air as from the ground, but there are a hundred other shades and shapes which are peculiar to their areas. Meanwhile, the more intimate features of the land will gradually replace the old conceptions of a roadside signpost. Thus the hulk of Arthur's Seat through the smoke haze up the Forth will fix the position of Edinburgh, and the shape of the islands in Loch Lomond will be a guide to Glasgow. Each on their day have provided the clue I needed. And there are many others – the loop of the river Mersey above Runcorn, the China Clay pyramids of north Cornwall, the Staines reservoirs on the approach to London from the south west, the tower at Blackpool, the gas meter at Heston, the white horse cut in the hillside over the Vale of Mowbray... all of them signposts on the highroads of the air. Such things take the place of the list of towns carried on a car journey, are more individual and easier to recognise. The shape of hills, as lovely as a dream and in bad weather very comforting to recognise, are graven on the airman's mind: the noble brow of the Wrekin for instance, or the bluff of Ralston Scar in Yorkshire. The rivers, too, assume a new character. You can not only see where they have come from and to where they are going, but they will frequently return the compliment when you have lost your way. I shall never forget the course of the Trent and the pale glint of the light on its water which once guided me for many miles on a day of appalling visibility, nor the sudden eastward sweep of the river Wyre one winter afternoon when the fog was stealing in from the Irish Sea. Lakes too have their shape, lakes most of all, for never two are the same and they shine large on the aerial map.

Yet beside such signs as these, there is the greater conception to be one of England as a whole. Before one has been flying for long, it is suddenly there in the mind like an arresting picture. While it can never be seen in actuality all at once, a surprising amount of it can bring the atlas to life with startling realism. I remember once finding myself at ten thousand feet over the Isle of Wight on a clear day. The whole of that area labelled on the school atlas, 'England, southern portion', was spread out beneath, from the sweep of the Cornish coast to the blue haze of the Lizard, round to the Thames estuary. If I couldn't actually see the holiday makers on the pier at Folkestone and the bathers on the beach at the Lizard, my eyes encompassed their little playgrounds. So in the same way have I seen the Welsh mountains and the Yorkshire moors by turning my head. It is hardly surprising that the flyer soon sees his native land in fresh terms. It becomes for him a triangle standing upon a noble base from Dover to the Lizard the whole of its right side almost fret; from hills, save for the purple lump in the north east marked as the Yorkshire moors. On the other side of the triangle he sees a vision which at first is confusing. There are high humps of land standing out in all directions, from the south west by Exmoor, to the extreme west by Wales, to the ragged masses of rock and earth which represent the Lake District; and in between is the long spine of the Pennines, and to the south the lesser swell of smaller ranges which might be perilous on a day of low lying clouds. But the confusion clears, just as the first shock of seeing the hundred dials in a modem bomber sorts itself into order.

In the centre of the triangle a circle can be drawn for the new flyer and painted red. Within it is the industrial belt, a land of gloom and generally foul flying weather. It contains Birmingham in the south, Liverpool in the west, Bradford in the north, and if there are no big industrial towns in the east, there is enough evidence of the others blown over by the prevalent west wind. Flying from London to Scotland, the east coast route impinges on the circle, and for nearly a hundred and fifty miles, from Bedford to Leeds, one may breathe the smoke blown across from the west. Just how heavy this can be during periods of atmospheric inversion (on many an overcast afternoon in the winter) has to be experienced to be believed.

Sometimes in a west wind it may be better to travel north by the western route. It is a lovely road on a fine day, carrying you over the Chilterns to Oxford, with glimpses of the Thames valley, and then over the Cotswolds into the fruit country by Evesham. It is a poor day on which the five hundred foot ridges of these wooded ranges are covered by cloud, and almost before you know it, you are changing course to a more northerly direction over the city of Worcester. Worcester is a good turning point, for you are now round the lower end of the Pennines and have a clear run up the Severn valley almost due north to pass eventually through the Warrington gap into the Lancashire plain. The Welsh hills rear their noble heads on the left, while on the right the stygian gloom is fed by the breath of Birmingham, Stafford, and Manchester, creating a line of darkness nearly a hundred miles long.

Of course the gap at Warrington no longer exists. But for four years it was a hole in the balloon barrage between Liverpool and the east Warrington, Manchester and the sprawling towns which lay about them. Many a time I had my last lateral view of the ground at the Nantwich salt works, still twenty miles from the gap, and have seen nothing until it was safely passed by another ten miles. It was necessary to steer a careful compass course and to check the track

as opportunity offered by peering vertically downwards in the hope of picking up some landmark. It was often the loop of the Mersey and sometimes an unbelievable chimney at Earlstown which belched so much smoke that even in that awful gloom it could be detected by the very darkness it created. Once the chimney had been located the bottleneck was passed, and it was probably not long before the watery sunshine would be glinting on the roofs of Southport a dozen miles away. Except for these minutes of anxiety, the route remains easy, continuing across the olive greens of the Lancashire plain up to the fringes of the Lake District by Kendal. If the clouds are down here, it may be best to cut across Morecambe Bay, to Millom, and to skirt the hills along the coast, past Whitehaven for the jump across the Solway Firth, and so round the coast of Wigtown into the Firth of Clyde. But sometimes even this will prove impossible. At such time I have flown up the Solway, sneaked across England through the Carlisle gap, and followed the valley of the Tyne and Hadrian's Wall to Newcastle. This is a well known back door by which one may often escape from bad weather into good on the east coast.

When the weather is fine the west provides an earlier whiff of the burns and braes which you are seeking. The sight of Arran lying like a vast rock in the central firth, and then successively the silver Kyles of Bute, Loch Striven, and finally the Gareloch are unfolding glories which the vast pall of smoke on your starboard hand only accentuates. The breath of Glasgow is no sweeter than Manchester's. Very soon you are over those islands at the south end of Loch Lomond, and if the Glasgow murk is sweeping this way, as it so often is, they are the necessary signpost to the north east and the Stirling valley. From now the road is open to Perth and the north.

Scotland, of course, is a less easy subject for a mental photograph. It has so many scars on its face, and in the west – from Arran to Cape Wrath, a distance of over two hundred miles as an aircraft flies – it is a wilderness of mountain ranges, sea lochs, rivers and islands, with scarcely a level field. A glimpse of ripening corn, or the soft greens common to English farmlands, are rarities. These western colours are silver and dark blue and burnt reds and old greys, and except for the hidden landing strips the whole area is as dangerous as it is attractive.

But the east coast has many of the characteristics of England – a level coastal fringe from Edinburgh to the Dornoch Firth. On days of poor flying weather the road to the Orkneys is by no means difficult, although the coastal route twists and turns prodigiously. But on clear days, the short cut across the mountains of the interior is worth taking, for nowhere in the world is the prospect finer.

Yet it is not for such delights that I write. But rather for the new conception of the land born of flying. It presents such an utterly different picture to the traveller that even the maps which he carries have had to be remade. The roads, for instance, have almost gone, reduced to thin lines of background. The towns have shrunk into insignificance and their names are printed in small letters. Instead, the woods spring out, delineated in bright green, their shapes faithfully recorded. The hills leap skywards in darkening shades of purple, and the lowlands are of a whiteness which admits of no other meaning. The lakes are a deep blue which startle the eyes and implant their shapes on the mind. Indeed, an air map is almost a picture which might be hung in a gallery. Only the darkly printed spider lines of the railways seem to mar its beauty. Of all manmade things, the railways alone stand out from the air. A great city can be missed beneath its pall of smoke, but not the lines which lead towards it. Even at night, the moon will glint on the metals and show them up.

Yes – a new conception of the land, and with its birth a new proprietorship over it. It allows a man to speak of Cornwall and the Orkneys in the same breath, and feel an equal kinship with the quiet southern rivers and the highland torrents. It might be true to say that we enter into our heritage with a deeper insight through this focus which we can bring to bear upon it. And now that the control column of an aeroplane is becoming no more strange than the handle of a fishing rod or the stock of a gun, it may be agreed that all three are not unnatural partners. For me at any rate they have been partners, and if I read the signs aright they will often be found travelling together in the future.

II

Just Fishing

On a summer evening in 1940, an evening of windless glory with the sky a flaming pageant, I met by the side of a south country chalk stream a very good fisherman. I saw him as I came up the bank on the lookout for a rising trout; he had his back to me as I moved from under the trees to a point where the river curved. There was hardly room to cast here, but there was a deep channel in the elbow of the river where a good fish might lie. It was with this corner that the fisherman was concerned. Wondering how he was going to propel his dry fly across the water without snagging it on the bushery behind, I paused and watched. He had to make a throw of nearly fifteen yards and if he could do it with a sideways cast, which seemed to be the only possible method, then he was a better fisherman than I.

I saw him lift his long line lightly off the water and then execute a Spey throw which left the line running out like a snake across the river. The cast was a joy to watch. The fly alighted on the far side in a patch of sunlight which came in over the tops of the trees, and floating for a moment, was suddenly the object of a commotion in the water. I saw the angler strike, and believed that his technique had had its just reward. But something went wrong... the fish rose short, or it was only pricked. At any rate the line leapt momentarily off the glassy surface to fall back in loose and useless coils. He reeled it in, shaking the gleaming water droplets from its loops until the fly was brought to his hand. It was then that he became aware of me.

'I made a mess of that one,' he said with a grin. 'Struck too soon.'

He was a younger man than I had thought, with a big mouth and wide, sensitive eyes.

'I've never seen the Spey throw used on a chalk stream,' I said. 'It made that cast possible – didn't it?'

He agreed that it was his show piece and that once in a while it caught him a fish which he wouldn't otherwise have had. With a shrug of his shoulders he nipped the barb of the fly into the cork handle and together we turned upstream, looking for possible new victims. We came to a break in the trees opening on to a water meadow where the sun fell in a golden slant. Here we looked down on a stretch of crystal water and stood for a while, waiting for some movement from a trout which would give us another chance. I wanted to see him demonstrate that throw again.

While we waited, talking of trout and of such matters as are of interest to fishermen the world over, the peace of the evening was suddenly shattered. A high whine from the supercharger of a Merlin engine cut through the still air, and, looking up, we saw the graceful shape of a Hurricane casting its silhouette against the sky. I had already seen so many aeroplanes that day, turning, wheeling, stuttering with their guns, that I didn't give it a second glance. But I noticed that my companion's eyes followed it and that on his face was a curious, animated, expression as though he was excited. His eyes followed it until it was out of sight, and then he drew a deep unconscious breath as though something disturbing had passed out of his mind.

'A Hurricane,' I said rather feebly.

'Good old Hurricane,' he echoed.

And then, of course, I knew. It was something in his voice which told me. He flew one himself, and when I asked him, he said that he and his squadron had been pretty busy these last few weeks. He'd got the afternoon off... the first afternoon he'd had for some while, though he'd been out with his rod after dark. He talked in a quiet, restrained voice, but I realised that his nerves were as taut as the skin of a drum. I changed the subject and we went back to our fishing.

He had a trout out of the smooth stretch in front of us before it grew dark, and I had a nice grayling out of the stickle at the top of it. But the fish weren't rising well that day, in spite of the hatch of duns which danced over the river. We fished on until the fingers of the searchlights began to probe the southern horizon, and then putting up our rods, walked together along the bank until we came to the bridge where, unknown to each other, we had hidden our cycles among the trees.

'Do you often come here?' I asked.

'Whenever I can,' he said. 'When things are quiet… I'll see you here again?'

I said that I hoped so, for I was on a course at a nearby aerodrome, and could get out most evenings. I had permission to fish this stretch, and it would be fun to make a joint assault on the river's trout. So we arranged to meet on the following Sunday.

He never came. Nor do I know what happened to him. But I am sure that he had been a better man because he came to the river to fish. This is the way of fishing.

If you have been afraid, and fear doesn't send you to sleep or to a party, it can do no better than send you to the banks of a river. The medicine is the sound of the water and the inevitability of its flow. The spirit of the river is greater than the spirit of man, and its overpowering strength finally anaesthetises the unquiet mind which comes within its influence. In time of war when good men can feel fear and still be good men, a night's fishing can bring everything again into true perspective. In peace, there is not the need to be fighting fear, but its place is taken by trivial worries, all of them magnified and doing their worst to take the freedom out of life. I have stood by the river in the gathering darkness, and as though I was passing through a door, have been taken into the night so that I became a part of it as much as the shadows. Out there where the water is flowing, there is no end and no beginning, but something which goes its way for ever in peace. The last smolts are perhaps dropping down the river to the sea, and the first adult sea-trout are going the other way, struggling up the rapid into the pool. In a few weeks the smolts will be exploring the ocean ledges for food, and their brothers of a generation ago will be ramming their noses up the furthest burn where they will spawn and start the cycle all over again. The salmon will be lying in its pool waiting for the spate which will give it room to navigate the next shallow, the last kelt of the season is dropping downstream, its survival still in the balance after its parenthood. Behind the rock in midstream, the big trout of the pool lies in wait for the flies the river brings it. This much we know, for it has risen three times in as many minutes. The coots have nested in the rushes again, hardly a foot above the water level, as though they knew that the river would not flood before their brood is fledged. The pair of wild duck which are bringing up a family somewhere in the thickets which line the bank have lighted to the flat below for a drink. It was to this flat that they brought the ducklings for their first swim. From far up the river comes a screech which can only belong to a heron, probably disturbed at his business by a fox. On the opposite shore a handful of pebbles rattle down the bank and fall with a plomp into the water, a piece of carelessness on the part of a water rat.

The man beside the river is a part of all this, and because it has no ending, he, too, assumes its immortality. For thus he returns to the river again and again.

The instinct to fish, to hunt, to lie quietly and observe the ways of nature, are dormant in most of us. They are apt to lie deeper with each succeeding generation as the lives of men are lived between higher and higher walls, and their excursions made in ever swifter transport. Then something awakes the instinct. Perhaps it is only curiosity, perhaps a desperate need for exercise. But one day it is suddenly insufficient to look down from the cabin of an aircraft at the unrolling hills, or through the unbreakable windows of a motorcar at the green fields on the other side of the hedge. You must stop, and go exploring as you did when you were a boy. Then lying on the bank of some stream, or looking up a valley in the gathering dusk, you see and hear the sounds of the unknown earth about you, and you are shocked at your ignorance of everything which sustains the life of the world.

From then on you may begin to hack a way out of the prison which you have built for yourself. Your friends may regard you as sick; you will not grow as rich as you believed you would, and the company of other men – some other men – will be less satisfying. Nearer at home, the metamorphosis of the man who discovers that there is a world around him is likely to lead to misunderstandings. To be kept late at the office is one thing, but to stay out half the night and return soaked to the skin, dirty and empty handed, is another. It may need more explaining than you have words at your command.

'Surely you're not going out again?' she said.

We were standing together looking through the window at the rain falling in long shafts against the background of the trees.

'I wish you wouldn't go,' she added. 'You know you'll never catch anything.'

It was probably true. But I had had a long spell at the controls of an aeroplane and I longed to get the smell of the burnt oil out of my nostrils.

So we looked into the dripping garden, and beyond it to where the wet sky hung low over the little town. Then to my mind came the picture of the river with a newly run sea trout jumping in a dark pool below the bridge.

I promised not to be late.

I had a fishing hut down by the river. It belonged to the railway company whose rightful tenant was the old man who looked after the level crossing at the end of the iron bridge. He came on duty at six o'clock and held his fort until the following morning. There was always a fire in the hut, fuelled by the driver of one of the northbound trains who each night slowed his engine to fling a few blocks of coal from the tender. By the time I arrived there was a blaze in the grate and a warm welcome. The old fellow used to leave his door open so that he could see down into the pool at the bottom of the bank and be able to give me an up-to-date report on the fish which were showing. He had even driven a post into the river, and took pride in reporting the movements of the water – whether it was rising or falling. And he warned off other fishermen, possibly with a better right to fish than I.

The rain had stopped when I reached the hut and there was a line of white light under the edge of the clouds along the western horizon. It looked as though, after all, it might be a fine night. Matthew came out to meet me, but as usual he refused to give me the information I wanted until I asked for it. It was an idiosyncrasy of his. He would talk about the trainloads of munitions which had been going past, or estimate the chances of the Russians halting the latest advances, and he would hang up my coat to dry. But he would never mention the fish.

When I tackled him he gathered up his voice at the bottom of his deep chest and growled to himself. 'What's that?' I said.

He repeated his mumblings:

'Just a chance – a nice chance perhaps.' But I wanted more information than that. 'Is the water rising?'

'It's not rising yet – it'll be another six or eight hours – maybe more.'

'And the fish,' I said. 'Have you seen any fish?'

The old man got up and slowly rolled himself out of the hut like a barrel.

'Come to the bridge,' he said.

So I followed him along the metals till we were leaning over the iron guardrail above the water. From here the pool lay directly below – a spit of shingle to the left that had been piled up by the current and a high bank to the right with an overhanging thorn bush. In behind the shingle, former floods had eaten out a deep pool which was turned into a swirling cauldron by the current rushing past. Then lower down the water was forced by the shingle towards the opposite side, and for nearly thirty yards it formed a smooth, deep glide before it widened again to break up over the lip of a shallow.

'There's a salmon this side of the thorn bush,' said Matthew. 'He's about two yards out where the current is heaviest. There's another in the narrow bit off the top of the spit – a smaller fish, and maybe a grilse. And there's a big sea-trout in beside him – I thought he was the grilse at first for they're both in the hole together where it's narrowest.'

As I looked down, the sea-trout jumped. He was certainly an un usually big fish for the river, although in the failing light he looked, perhaps, heavier than he really was.

'Have you seen anything in the glide?' I asked.

'Can't say that I have,' said the old man reluctantly; 'but there's bound to be a few sea-trout ... bound to be. Duncan was telling me they've been running and Henderson has had them in the nets this past week.'

It was dark by the time I slithered down the embankment on the far side of the bridge. The pool fished from this side, and best of all off the spit into the smooth glide. It meant leaving the top salmon alone, for it lay higher than the cauldron and across on the far side.

When I got on to the spit, there was little to be seen save the dividing line between the shingle and the water at my feet. Only the top of the thorn bush thirty yards away cast the outline of its foliage against the sky. Beneath it, and downstream of where I was to pitch my flies, was a well of utter blackness. The firelight of old Matthew's hut was still in my eyes, and they would take another twenty minutes to become night adapted. Not that it mattered, for the shape of the pool, from the piers of the bridge to the step of the run fifty yards below, was graven on my mind.

I was using ten feet of artificial gut tonight, which did not make my task any easier. Japanese gut never goes out well, although the heavy flies on the tail and bob would help it. There had been a local shortage of genuine gut, and I had pulled off a few yards from my fixed spool spinning reel.

I tried the grilse and the sea-trout, which were distant no more than a flick of the wrist from where I was crouching. It was impossible to see where the flies went, but I knew that they were within a dozen feet of me. As they drifted down and across for a second time, there was a big splash and a drop of water fell on my cheek. But the flies were already below the fish, and had had nothing to do with the movement. Nor would the fish look at the flies on a second cast.

It now became necessary to get out an increasingly long line and cover more and more of the glide below. Once there was a check, but it was only the bank on the further side. I had pulled out a foot too much line.

The water was making a merry noise over the stones, and a dull roar came up from the fast run below. I heard a splash under the far bank, although I saw nothing. By the time I had reached it, I thought that I was going to have another blank night. There was only a couple of yards of good water left – a glassy channel in the far corner before the water broke. This necessitated a really long cast in the darkness, and accuracy would have been impossible if I hadn't known the pool. I put all I knew into the following throw, and a couple of seconds later was sure that I had overdone it. There was a check, just as there had been when the fly was caught in the bank. But banks don't move, and my fly did. I was into a fish – and with a lightning rush across the stream it came towards me and jumped.

I could see the silver drops of the water as they fell back like an explosion of dim light. Looking up, I noticed that there were more stars overhead. It was a good fish – as they so often are in this corner – and as a precaution I drowned the line by holding the rod low over the water. Simultaneously, I backed along the spit upstream in the hope that he would follow me. I had known sea-trout to bolt down the rapid when they were not well clear of the spit, and its passage on a dark night was worse for the fisherman than it was for the fish.

While I was playing him, a train thundered over the bridge, its firebox flinging a brilliant glow against a plume of smoke. The noise of it drowned all other sounds, and forced my attention from the river so that my eyes were now held by the flat trucks flickering past against the stars. When it had gone, the fish had gone, too. It was a strange thing, for the line was in the middle of the glide and I had felt no change in the strain. The trout had just melted away, apparently leaving the hook lightly wedged under a stone. When it was pulled, it came away, and on reeling it in and turning on the torch, I saw it was unmarked.

A full hour had passed since I began to fish, and I reckoned it to be the best hour – the first after nightfall.

But I needn't have worried.

Before the blink of the false dawn threw up the shapes of the trees and painted the river with its cold grey wash, I was to have six heavy trout in my bag – and every one of them out of the glide I had just fished with so little success. Before I went I was to see the first of a new run of trout scrambling up the shallow and entering the pool as the water began to rise – just as Matthew had said.

It sometimes happens this way, and I think it is the combination of a change in the weather and a coming rise of the water. By two o'clock the rain clouds had dissolved and it was a brilliant starlit night over a scattering of stratocumulus. The temperature remained high, and this no doubt kept away the dawn mist from the water – this and a gentle westerly which blew across the meadows.

The first fish was the big one from the pot and the best I ever had from the river. I had to look at him closely on the following morning before I was convinced he was a sea-trout, for although he only weighed five and a half pounds he was far above the average for the river and more in keeping with the grilse.

It must have been nearly three o'clock when he and his brethren decided to come to the top and feed; and between that moment and first light, there was scarcely a minute when the surface somewhere on the glide was not broken. It confirmed a theory that it is scarcely worth changing the lures when fishing for sea-trout at night that it is better to fish on until the trout begin to move. Then they will grab at anything which comes their way – salmon flies, loch flies, demons, terrors, flashy tags of tinsel – anything.

The sport of playing a big sea-trout at night is as much as my nerves will stand. I have so often laboured until my muscles ached for no reward, and then at last got into a big one – a far bigger one than would have been bearable to lose. Tonight this fine trout drew the rod into a bow and sent its vibrations up the line, unseen, unheard, but immensely powerful. When he turned and ran down the pool with the speed of a salmon, there seemed to be little chance of getting him out; and there was always the depressing thought that however careful you may be, two out of every five sea-trout get away. It is perhaps the softness of their mouths and the electric qualities of their fighting which make them so difficult in the dark.

Three times on the way down the pool I held my ground and fought him to a standstill, but each time he came nearer to the shallow rapid. And then suddenly he was into it, and I was stumbling over the stones in pursuit, doing everything to keep the lightest strain on him, and at the same time to hold the rod high so that the cast should clear the snags. It was only luck which brought us both together again in the quiet pool below. We were a hundred and fifty yards away from the glide where he had been hooked, and I was standing in two feet of motionless backwater on a sandy bottom, peering out across the black surface in the hope of discovering where in the darkness the fish might be. The strain was as great as the little rod could bear, and it seemed as if he must surrender in a few minutes. But it was not until I got below him another fifty yards downstream that it was possible to work him into the side; and then he made a surprising jump on a short line and really deserved to get away. His whole weight fell across the cast and smashed the rod down on to the water. Amazingly, the cast held. When I had a glimpse of him a moment later in the beam of the torch, he was coming in towards the bank tail first, steadily, as though he was drowning.

There was a narrow beach at my feet, and I pulled him gently on to it to find that the cast was twice round his tail and jammed. The hook was still in the angle of his jaw, but it had all but torn through the tendons. The chance of getting him out had he not looped the cast round his tail as he jumped would have been slender indeed.

I walked slowly back to the head of the glide through the field, not worrying whether I never saw another fish. By the weight of the bag I knew that I had caught the biggest sea-trout I had had for a long time. I went back to the same place, cast again, and was into

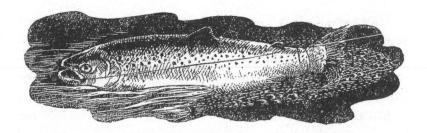

another fish within five minutes. After the first one, it seemed a sprat. I never moved as I played out its life. Then another was landed, and two more lost before I took a couple of paces downstream to cover fresh water. There was now a pluck at almost every cast. The flies were drifting twenty yards out in the darkness, moving slowly across the current. Only a splash denoted a rising fish. The first suggestion of dawn was in the sky when I caught the last one. He came from the corner where I had lost the first; and he was a beauty of two and a half pounds.

Old Matthew's face was a study in shades of pleasure when he saw the bag. 'I knew we'd get fish tonight,' he said, and then he hurried on to give me orders about returning tomorrow – or rather, that evening – and getting some more. But honour was satisfied, and Matthew had to be content with the two and a half pounder to take home across the handlebars of his cycle when he went off duty.

Six sea-trout weighing fifteen pounds was one of the best catches I have had, and if I live to be a hundred I shall never ask anything more of a night's fishing. They looked well on the breakfast table. The rashness of setting out in the rain of the previous night was justified, while she who would have had me stay at home said that I was a great fisherman.

Four hours later I was crossing the coast in an aircraft and heading out over the North Sea. The sun was pouring into the cockpit, brightening the yellow collar of my Mae West so that it shone like gold. The instrument panel was in shadow, but the white figures of the dials gleamed like the eyes of benevolent ghosts. The coast and the world of rivers and fish grew smaller and smaller, but the drone of the engine was a soporific so that the mind remained amongst them, half drugged, to relive the triumphs of the night. Only when the ring of the directional gyro swung a degree or two off course was I reminded by the observer that I was supposed to be working.

These days and nights almost persuaded me that it was practicable to burn the candle at both ends. The exercise taken along the banks of the river in the shimmering darkness counterbalanced the lack of sleep.

There was another pool I fished. It was even better than the one lying close to the river's mouth, although when I saw it for the first time it looked hopeless. It was one of those places where one knew there must be trout, and probably plenty of them. But it was almost equally certain that they would prove uncatchable. It lay in one of the higher reaches of the river – a glassy deep which slid quietly over shelves of rock and between the high walls of a gloomy canyon. The sea-trout usually reached it by the end of July, and it offered them a wonderful harbour after the stormy passage of the middle river. They had come through a chain of rapids with foam flecked rocks and vicious little falls, a stiff ascent in any state of the water. The instinct which warns migratory fish of their difficulties, no doubt told them that above this resting place there was an even rougher road. So they spread themselves out through the crystal quiet of the rock pools and waited. Overhead was a tunnel of trees through which the sun plunged in vertical shafts. Looking down into the water, in places over ten feet deep, the bottom stood out as though under a magnifying glass. There were underwater cliffs with blue shadows and miniature caves made by their overhang – places with sharp edges to cut a cast. But it was the clearness of the water which made the gorge appear so impossible.

In the widest pool, where the river moved with slow majesty over shelving rocks, the sea-trout could be seen lying as dark shapes, motionless, as though held in a transparent jelly. You had to approach slowly between the rocks and under the branches of the trees or else they would see you and dart away like a flicker of silver light. But when the sun was behind a cloud, and if you crawled an inch at a time to the head of the pool where the ledges crushed the river into a narrow channel, you could sometimes get close to them and find yourself looking down on a dozen sea-trout. The catching of one of them under such conditions was a fisherman's nightmare.

But at night, making your way from the bridge through the fields, and then dropping down to the river at the head of the gorge, you would see a very different picture. The remains of the light would be drained away, and then the grumbling of the water above would be lost in a new quiet. In its place would come the sound of splashing fish and you'd know that every pool in the chain had become alive. On a warm summer night it gave the impression of entering a treasure chamber, for in the filtered starlight the corners of the rocks looked like the bound chests of a pirate's plunder. It was no use arriving before starlight. If the sun was still on the mountain tops, or even if the clouds were still pink in the afterglow, it was too early. Then it was best to follow along the river till you came to the bend half a mile up, and to fish the swift current under the opposite bank. A salmon might be lying there, and as the light failed there was a chance of a sea-trout at the tail of the pool. In the gorge itself, stealth was needed, even after nightfall. The trout had a knack of detecting your presence, perhaps through the vibration of hobnailed boots on the hard rock. They could be put down by a sudden movement, and if it was followed by a clumsy cast, it might be the last you would see of them.

Here in the gorge, I remember a night of slow crawling to the river's edge, with the light of the stars filtering through the trees and the splash of trout coming out of the well of darkness ahead. I sat down on a ledge which dropped sheer into ten feet of water at the neck of the pool. An hour before I had crept a foot at a time to the same position, and lying full length on the slab had marked the inhabitants of the water. There was a salmon within six feet of me unless he had moved, and just behind him a sea-trout of noble dimensions. Down the pool for a distance of twenty yards, I had counted another fifteen fish. Some of them were now splashing in the darkness, and as I felt for the fly, pinned to the cork handle of the rod, it seemed certain that I must hook one of them.

I pulled out a yard or two of line, hung it upstream, and lowered it into the river. I was thinking of the big sea-trout which had been lying behind the salmon. I sensed the fly swing in towards the ledge at my feet. Nothing happened. I lifted it, and swam it again down to the narrow neck. This time there was a sensational snatch, followed instantly by an explosion of water under my nose. It was as though the surface of the river had opened to release the pent up forces of a projectile. The splash which followed showered me with droplets. I could feel their sting on my cheek and on the backs of my hands. Then there was silence again, save for the occasional fish rising lower down the pool. The line was hanging slack.

I reached out and ran my fingers down the cast. The fly was still there. I thought of the things I had heard about salmon not taking a fly at night, and doubted them. In my mind's eye was a picture of the big sea-trout. I imagined him jumping out of the water and falling back again, and however I exaggerated the mental image, I couldn't create a splash as big as the one which had just showered me with water.

I lit a pipe, puffed at it for a while, and then tried another cast, recriminating with myself...why hadn't I lowered the point of the rod...why hadn't I cast from further back when there would have been some slack line to absorb the shock. The self-imposed examination nearly cost me a second fish, for suddenly the rod jerked and the reel went out. The strain was so heavy that I gave up my intention of playing the fish from where I was. It might be the last one I hooked, and if I disturbed the rest of the pool, I should at least have a better chance of taking this one home.

So I lowered the rod and drowned the line, and getting to my feet, felt my way over the rocks downstream. It was then that I realised that the fish was already out of the pool. It had passed through the narrow gateway at its lower end, and was now in the deep water of the next. The line was running over the side of its guardian rock and my first concern was to shift it clear and regain direct contact.

The only way to do it was to peel the line from the reel until the strain came off the fish, and then to throw it upwards and outwards over the rock. At the third attempt I succeeded and began to tighten up in the hope of finishing the fight early. But the trout seemed to possess unusual cunning, for while I had been busy it had returned to the pool in which it was hooked, and again I had to throw the line over the intervening rock, this time in the reverse direction. At last I had the fish tight again, and followed it slowly to the head of the pool where I had been sitting originally. There in the neck of water, within a yard of where I had started, I gaffed him by the beam of the torch. He weighed just over four pounds.

Two pools had been disturbed, and though trout continued to rise, both below and above, I failed to hook one securely. An irritating pluck and a slack line were my only rewards. Yet I had my monster, and memories of another. It was enough. The run home that night under the paling stars banished any regrets – together with the aches from my arms and back. The warm wind which never grew chill with the approach of dawn seemed to be the breath of life itself. If the mountains around me slept, this wind lived and laughed. I still seemed to breathe it as I crept into bed beneath an open window.

Today as I am writing, the grey clouds are driving in from the sea on a south easterly gale. There is a sting of rain in the air, which the glow of the fire is doing its best to make us forget. On the other side of the fireplace the Commander is turning over the paper. His face is wind tanned and he looks as though he were not yet dry. He has been fishing. In the corner behind me, the Chaplain is busy cataloguing the library books. He has just informed me that as soon as he has finished he is cycling ten miles to the burn which flows into the bay up the coast – he wants to know whether I will accompany him. I tell him that I should have been delighted if I hadn't been on duty. Two hours ago, I made up a cast for a friend who had travelled four hundred miles so that he could spend five days' leave on the local rivers and lochs. Four of the days have already gone by, and he has had only three fish. If he catches nothing today, he will still travel four hundred miles back to his ship feeling satisfied.

Fishermen all – perhaps not fully understood by the other occupants of the leather chairs in this big room, perhaps regarded with suspicion as men with manias. That south easterly gale which tugs at the window frames is no zephyr to make the Chaplain's ride a pleasure, or the prospect of the Commander's shave before dinner more than a painful duty.

Why do we do it – why do so many of us in the remote places to which lucky circumstance has banished us take such liberties with our comfort? The flying Commander refers to our activities as 'the fishing racket', as though it was indecent and probably illegal. The First Lieutenant reserves his spoken comments to gravely uttered congratulations when one of us catches a salmon, but the tone of his voice is one which he might equally use were we recovered from an unmentionable disease. The Captain is pleased to accept a cut from a fish and has been known to inquire how it is done. But one and all make us feel that we are doing something which is outside the true sphere of civilised human beings. There is no final diagnosis for our cases, and certainly no cure. But the tag end of a conversation at lunch perhaps provides a clue. Someone said, 'I don't understand why you old men don't give up flying… isn't it about time?'

It is – but we like it.

III

After the Gale

There had been a gale from the south west. By the late afternoon I had decided that I never wanted to see an aeroplane again. The five tons of metal which I had been flying had been tossed around like a cork in a three dimensional mill stream, so that by the time I had battered my way back across the coast and seen the friendly land below I would have admitted to anyone that my flying days were numbered.

At about five o'clock the gale died. It was as though the breath had been expelled from the lungs of a dragon. There was a sudden quiet, so that people looked up and said with surprise 'It's gone'. At six o'clock there was not a breath. The pines which overshadowed the gate cut a black pattern against the clearing sky and the clang of four bells could be heard a mile away. But my internal mechanism still protested and my mind fretted. It was a case for the antidote which lay nearest. It was reached by a swift passage to a place where the prettiest and gamest of loch trout abounded.

The distance was nine miles. It lay along a winding lane heavy with pine woods, and then across a brief waste of scrub and bracken.

At the end of it there was a new forest of pine, and a lane which disappeared among the trees. If you followed it, you would, after a while, burst out into the sun and find yourself in a ring of trees like the clasp of a jewel of which this was the centre. Within the ring was a reservoir whose beauty deserved a better word.

I had found it originally from the air, a gleam of water which on this first occasion served as no more than a useful pinpoint. But the olive roof of its tree tops and the glancing silver of the water, and then suddenly the little tongues of flaming colour which came leaping from a grassy bank and were probably rhododendrons, decided one to return. The chance actually came a couple of hours later when with a job done and the wireless aerial safely wound in, I made a low level attack.

I flew up a dell fresh with young bracken, and lifted the aircraft over the barrier of guardian pines. A few hundred yards of trees sped beneath the wings, their tips left rocking in the rude blast. Then letting her drop, we skimmed the slippery silver of a water channel lined by magnificent firs. On the one hand was a low embankment of clipped turf, lit by those flaming rhododendrons which I had seen earlier. Below the embankment, girded by a new apron of lawn, a grey roofed house was sunk into the background of the trees, a flash of gravel by its front door. On the other side of the water the trees crowded down to the edge, their feet lined by a fringe of gorse.

After a few hundred yards – a few seconds of watchful flight – the channel divided right and left, and the trees grew closer together until a swift tug at the control column shot us clear of their crests. Circling and taking a new look at the loch, I saw that the channels which had sprung out from the main lead encircled an island, an island shaped like a triangle whose apex divided the waters. Opposite the base of the island, on the far side, was another short lead of water ending abruptly in the wall of trees.

After one more run, this time with my eyes on the house (a man was now standing at the door) I climbed, and looked for roads which would bring me back to this well concealed glen.

Ten minutes afterwards I landed, and within another ten minutes was poring over a one inch map. This was another day on which my reaction to flying set in with immediate results. I was soon making the swift passage under the trees and into the inner ring where I had seen the house, and just in case, a trout rod and haversack with cast box, flies and reel were slung over my shoulder. There was good reason to believe that they might come in useful, for the map had marked the place as a reservoir, and reservoirs in these parts usually contained fish.

The man came out to meet me, and I deliberately flashed the gold buttons of my uniform with the idea of suggesting that I was a stray with no dishonest intentions. This was accepted, and removing the remainder of much motorcycling equipment (there was a friendly invitation in the man's eyes) I played the opening gambit.

'I saw your place today,' I said, 'and then I looked it up and came along – it occurred to me that there might be some fish in it.'

The man was looking at me steadily – bright brown eyes under the peak of a tweed cap. He was a splendid gamekeeper type, lean and intelligent, with strong hands and an easy stance.

'You wouldn't be the chap who came over here in an aeroplane, would you?' he said.

'An aeroplane?' I echoed, thinking that my chances of fishing were rapidly departing. 'Which aeroplane?'

Then he smiled, and I knew it was all right.

'By God,' he exploded. 'I thought the roof was coming off – you had yon trees standing over like there was a gale of wind – mon, but you was low!'

'I'm sorry,' I said meekly. 'I won't do it again.'

'Come inside,' he said, turning on his heel – and I followed him. We went through the back door into a dark passage and stopped by a little table with a book on it. 'That's the fishing book,' he said. 'Sign it.'

I signed hurriedly.

'You'll find the fish run up to a pound and a quarter – and it's no' a bad night – you ought to get a few.'

So I came back here time after time and grew to love it. It was a place of escape without harsh sounds or bustle. It is strange how such things can appeal to one who for the other half of life prefers speed and noise.

Tonight I made the familiar journey through the archway of trees and found Angus standing on the top of the bank, his figure bathed in sunshine, as though he had been waiting for me.

'So you're going to have a shot at them?' he said. I nodded and asked the chances.

'It's queer – but there's been two baits out, and they've had only one fish between them all day. Och, but you never know!'

Angus had a slow way of speaking. Often he didn't answer a question for a long while as he stood motionless looking out over his loch, seeing the flaming chaplet of gorse on the far bank, the green wall of trees, the brushwood duck hides on the island, or perhaps searching the rippled water for a sign of a rise. He was a magnificent fisherman himself, with a style of his own, and sometimes when I wanted a trout to take home he would go specially to fetch his rod, and then with a dark smile go down to the water by the landing stage and catch me one. He fished with a long straight line – against all my own beliefs – and would bring in his flies in short, quick jerks, recovering his line only a few inches at a time between his fingers.

I remember once how I had bargained with my Squadron Commander for an afternoon off in return for supplying seven trout to be served that night at the squadron dinner, and how by six o'clock with only an hour to go I still had four trout to catch. It was Angus who had come to the rescue with that quick, deadly action of his. I don't believe it would have worked on all waters – but it produced in the course of a visit to his favourite places the missing fish. At two minutes to seven I delivered the goods.

'So you don't think I'll do any good tonight?' I repeated.

He looked up into the eye of a newly lisping breeze, and said with a tone of finality, 'I had a cast down the embankment half an hour ago – and I never saw a fish.'

I was, however, a bigger optimist than most. An evening ripple was spreading over the water, and although there wasn't a sign of trout, I had an idea that I was going to catch one, even though the method might not be orthodox.

There are more ways of catching trout in a loch than flogging the surface. Hunched in the stern of a boat, casting through the long day until your wrists ache, neither seeing a rise nor touching a fish, is a misuse of other and perhaps better opportunities. When fish are not on the surface, it is sometimes impossible to make them rise; in fact, it is doubtful whether the flies are seen by the trout.

At such times – and the evening of which I write was perhaps one of them – the fish are at the bottom of the loch. They are not in the smoky depths like submarines sheltering from a depth charge attack, but they are in that area generally termed the shallows, limited perhaps to ten or twelve feet of water. They may be feeding on larvae, nymphs, bloodworms, grubs or whatever food may be on offer among the weeds or the stones which line the bottom. Or they may be just hanging around doing nothing... there is little evidence one way or the other. But one thing emerges with certainty – and that is the futility of trailing flies across the top of the water. The fisherman who goes on casting hopefully, changing his flies every quarter of an hour in the belief that he will eventually find something which will be taken, is a gallant optimist. I have found it pays better to reserve one's energy, backing the probability of an evening rise and waiting for it.

When you have made the journey to the water as I had done this night, and found conditions apparently hopeless, there are, however, one or two things which you can try, and sometimes they produce surprising results. It was with this end in view that I declined the offer of a boat and trudged westwards up the bank.

I came opposite the island and continued through the trees, more widely spaced here and standing back a little from a high heather bank. A breath of wind filtered into the channel and rippled the fifty yards of water which separated me from the island. Down the opposite bank one of the two boats was making a drift, and as I passed I called out and asked whether they had had any luck. The answer was depressing. They had not seen a trout move for two hours.

At the head of the channel was a little bay which shallowed out to a few inches of water – a good place on a warm June evening. Off its point the loch deepened, and it was here that I began to fish. It took a few minutes to soak the line – a necessity for the employment of the ensuing tactics. Then using all the power in the rod, I got the flies perhaps twenty yards out into the loch... a crosswind cast born of brute force. Then I sat down on a big clump of heather and filled a pipe. After it was filled, but before it was lit, I judged the time was ripe to do some more work. The line had disappeared, the flies were perhaps six feet down ...perhaps on the bottom and snagged. There were risks to this game, but they had to be taken.

Within a matter of seconds it was clear that everything was well... the line was free. Now holding the rod point low on the water, and at just a sufficient angle for the tip to absorb the shock should a fish take, I began to recover the flies in swift, short jerks. I think that about six inches of line were coming in with each act of recovery, and that their frequency was in the neighbourhood of half a second to each. It was Angus's own method, save that the flies were fished very much deeper.

A couple of yards had come in – not more – when there was a check... a distinctive pluck like a sea-trout's gambit when it has toyed with a lure without taking it into its mouth. Policy on these occasions is to do nothing except to continue with the recovery. A yard or two later there was another pluck, and this time it was a good one. The strain remained, and with a sideways flick of the rod, the point bent and a fish was on. It was almost certainly the same fish which a second before had made the first half hearted offer.

In half a minute it came to the surface, jumped, and started to fight in earnest. The line was torn off for a few yards, and the pawl of the reel buzzed. I looked up the channel to where the boat was still in the course of its drift a hundred yards away. It was gratifying to see the white orbs of two faces turned in my direction. They had heard the reel, and were watching, doubtless with thwarted sentiments. How stupid and childish it was, but how pleasant to have one's trick work at the first cast!

The fight was soon over, and a silvery Loch Leven trout of three quarters of a pound was on the bank. I laid it on the heather where the sunlight played on its side and revelled in smug satisfaction. Then for a moment I sat contented, listening to the dip of the oars from the boat. The party were returning to the head of the channel, evidently convinced that a rise had started at my end. I waited for them, and soon they were level with me. The boat was turned

across the wind, just out of the reach of my longest cast, and a new drift was begun. Then I picked up my own rod.

Half a dozen casts later – for each of which I laid down the rod, put my hands in my pockets, stretched, and yawned while the flies sank – another trout took a firm hold. Once again I played a fish, and within a few minutes successfully landed him. He was a little smaller.

'What flies are you using?' came a shout from the boat. 'They are taking a Hardy's Gold Butcher,' I sang out.

One of the rods was withdrawn, and no doubt a Hardy's Gold Butcher found its way on to a dropper. The other rod continued to ply the water, if possible at increased speed.

While the boat drifted another twenty yards, a third fish took a fly and was duly landed. It was a half pounder. I thought I was going to have a record evening – although like my other good starts, the sport slacked off as time went on. Yet in just over an hour, I had six fish on the bank, and at a conservative estimate a dozen more had been pricked. Meanwhile, the boat had made two more drifts along the same bank, and on each occasion its occupants fished the water which I later covered myself. They had no luck.

The moral of this story leads nowhere. If there is an excuse for telling it, it is the suggestion it implies – that similar tactics are worth trying when everything else fails. But it should be admitted that it doesn't always work. Perhaps on two occasions out of five fish will take flies worked in this way through comparatively deep water. But even then – as far as my own experience goes – the method shows better results in the earlier part of the year. I never remember doing much with it after the end of June. The water on each occasion has been clear, generally between five and nine feet deep, and warm. Its lack of success later on perhaps has something to do with the increasing cloudiness of the water which on many lochs becomes a kind of thin green soup through millions of suspended weed particles. Nor has the method often worked from a boat. It seems as though it is best to recover the cast from the deep water into the shallow, the fish striking at a fly two or three times in the course of a single cast. As this implies, far more fish are pricked than are securely hooked, but this is the natural way of all long lines.

If no results are achieved at first, the flies can be sunk to varying depths, until they finally snag the bottom or a fish. A lead shot might be useful to get them down, although whenever I have tried it, I have never caught a fish.

The pattern of the flies doesn't seem to matter. I have a high regard for a Grouse and Green and Hardy's Gold Butcher; but I've done just as well on other flies, and particularly on a small Peacock demon. There was one particular demon which I used for years and which in spite of it being a little tattered is still on the active list. It is dressed on two low water salmon irons, but instead of a silver tinsel body, the silver is painted on with nail varnish.

The theory is logical and elementary. The trout are not on the surface, and to reach them the flies, lures, or whatever are used, must accordingly be sunk. By holding the rod point low, and if necessary actually below the surface, they can be 'worked' deep. The principle is not unlike the tactics one would use against salmon in deep pools in the early spring. The short, sharp jerks seem to be an advantage and to interest more fish. But there is so much line out that the movement of the flies themselves must be much smoother than the actions at the angler's end. The belly of the line, too, absorbs much of the shock in striking from a rod which is held pointing down the line.

Angus was waiting for me at the landing stage. The sun had set and the breeze was now only a whisper. Across the loch the last of the boats was coming in, oars rising and dipping to the click of the rowlocks. As we waited for the boat, Angus asked whether I had done any good, and I opened my haversack. A smile spread over his mahogany face, and he commented on the first of the fish... it had a grand small head and was deep in the girth. He asked me how I had got them, and I told him. His interest was less than I expected, but he asked that I should give him a demonstration. So I freed the line and cast far out into the calm water, put the rod down, and waited. When I picked up the rod the cast was fast on the bottom.

'There might be a few fish rising the night,' said Angus when the last of the visitors had gone. I shook my head in answer to the implied suggestion, but when he invited me to have supper with him, and said he would take a cast himself when it was really dark, my reluctance vanished. When Angus comes out, things happen.

So in the rosy glow of a flickering fire and a pool of soft light from an oil lamp on a spotless cloth, and to the tune of subdued voices, I sat down before two boiled eggs, thick hunks of new bread, and strong tea. There are worse things on a June night.

We talked of fruit and its bottling, of strawberries which Mrs Angus cultivated in profusion, principally because Angus had a secret and hitherto unsuspected passion for them, strange taste in a Scotch keeper, and of the war and its probable ending, and then we stretched ourselves and went out into the starlight, pipes glowing, and feeling that we were on the brink of adventure.

'Bank or boat?' I asked.

'We'll tak' the boat,' said Angus, and the rattle of its chain rang on the stone embankment as he eased the moorings.

A few fish were rising, the rings glinting here and there in the quarter light. The shadow of an owl flickered overhead and we heard the thick whir of its wings. Somewhere in the distance partridges were cheeping.

In a few minutes the quiet dip of the oars was sending us over the loch to the far bank, to the gorse at the foot of the trees. The night had put out their flames and only black shadows leaned over the water. Close in some heavy fish were rising, unseen, but noisy.

'Try a cast in under the bushes,' said Angus.

So it was that we began to fish. Nor had we to wait long, for the tempo of a wonderful evening rise increased every minute, and for an hour the boat crept like a ghost a yard at a time within the shadows. It was once again an example of the way trout will come up on a warm night after a day of almost complete inactivity.

Our fishing methods differed as chalk from cheese. Angus in the bows used his long line and his quick, jerky recovery, so much like the method I had used earlier in the evening, save that his flies were always near the surface. On the other hand, my own line was barely more than the length of the rod, and the big flies were made to swim slowly through the water in broad arcs. Fish came to both of us, but more to Angus. Yet while Angus had more rises, he pricked and lost twice as many fish, while I with my short line rose fewer but hooked more.

We were both murderous in our tactics, and I doubt whether one big trout which fell to my companion took more than thirty seconds to net. It weighed a pound and a quarter. The fish were rising right under the bushes where there could not have been more than twelve inches of water. Occasional rises came from further out, but the best trout seemed to be close in against the dark bank. One of them which we surprised was little better than beached when it took the fly… took it as it alighted on the surface and then made a desperate scramble to get into deeper water.

It was a fitting finish to an unusual day. Between us we brought into the landing stage nine trout weighing over eight pounds and we had been out a mere ninety minutes. As the chain was once more slipped through the ring in the bows there came from the east, high up against the stars, the throb of aero engines. They came nearer and nearer until their drumming was overhead. We strained our eyes into the infinity of the spangled sky, but it seemed as remote and as empty as ever.

'Glasgow'll be getting it tonight,' said Angus.

IV

By Air to the North

S ooner or later a pilot, whether serving at sea or at a shore base, ran the risk of receiving an invitation for duty in Whitehall. It was an invitation which was impossible to refuse, and when it came it meant putting away flying kit, fishing rods, guns, and perhaps much else which had been regarded as important. It meant bringing out a shiny monkey jacket to hang on a nail behind an office door, and was followed by a shopping expedition for a piece of felt to tie down on to the seat of a hard chair. These and other designs for economy thereafter ruled the struggle for existence, until the appointments branch could be persuaded to see reason.

For a long time I had avoided appointments which might have taken me away from practical flying – which meant equally from an outdoor life. It was a happy circumstance that an aircrew's hours of business were short, and if they happened to be shore based there was little objection to any plan which involved the capture of a salmon after other engagements had been discharged. One autumn, however, the long delayed invitation arrived and I found

myself in London with a ground job. Yet it was this which was to
persuade me finally that an aeroplane and a fishing rod had the
closest affinity. The job required me from time to time to visit our
widely scattered bases, and the discovery of a communications
flight established at a London aerodrome provided the means. From
here I catapulted myself across England and Scotland at startling
speeds, and if the aircraft I flew happened to carry a fishing rod or
a gun, as well as a briefcase, it was nobody's business but my own.
Those swift journeys which began in the Piccadilly tube on fine
mornings and ended an hour or so later in Cornwall, or in Scotland,
were undoubtedly the forerunners of thousands of others which will
be made in the years to come.

Shortly before Whitehall lost the last of its remaining charms
– through its shrieking whistles which gave its inhabitants fifteen
seconds to get under their desks – I made a journey which I shall
long remember, for it began with a minor disaster and ended with
some unusual luck. The disaster was of the elementary kind – I
left my salmon flies behind. Then after landing three hours out
of London it began to rain. It rained for fifty-two hours, while the
contents of my briefcase became more and more attenuated and I
feared that my legitimate business would be done before the river
fell to a fishable level. The rain was putting an end to a drought
which had lasted through February and March, so that the river had
remained at its summer level, preventing the run of the spring fish.

The storm in the hills was like the tuning up of a great orchestra.
First it was a mere tinkle, and then with an increasing volume the
flood mounted until the burns were torrents which tossed white
spray over their boulders. The dross from the previous year began
to come down and then an offering from the new – the body of a

newly born lamb. Broken fence timbers, the branches of trees, and straw from the valley farms, swirled and tossed in the high water.

The biggest salmon flies would have been useless – although in a few hours, so quickly do the little rivers run away, even small flies might catch fish. A friend came to my rescue with a box of sixty salmon flies which he had just been given, and when I opened the case I blinked into a sunset of gaudy colours which would have gladdened any salmon fisherman's heart. But a second later I saw that the flies had gut eyes, and worse, that they were rotten. Instead of bright opaque loops, the gut was yellow with age, brittle, and useless. The gaudy bodies, and hackles of blousy, overdressed brilliance – Golden Pheasant, Indian Crow, Turkey, Teal, Jungle Cock, Swan and Peacock in profusion, were in the fashion of twenty or thirty years ago. It was a point of little account to a man with a pair of scissors, for they could be thinned, but the gut eyes – what a risk I should be taking!

I chose four of them, snicked them into my trout box, and then, while the rain was still falling, went trout fishing on a little loch in the hills. It couldn't rain forever.

On the third day the nimbostratus clouds rolled away and the sun came out, and all around the tops of the mountains grew out of the sky like a photograph developing. It was time to go down the valley for a salmon. But first I rang up my host to confirm the prospects.

'The river's down to twenty-six,' he said, 'and clearing rapidly.' (He was referring to the level of his gauge.) 'It ought to be a good fly water tomorrow.'

But he added a warning. There had been fish in the river before the flood, but a raid had been made by poachers on the lower pools upon which he was relying to stock his own water. Worse – over two hundred clean salmon had been picked out, poisoned, down by the mouth of the river. There was a court case on about it – though little satisfaction was to be had from that. Two hundred fish poisoned and more dynamited by poachers was a heavy loss for a little river, and there had been no salmon safe in the middle reaches before either disaster.

I met my host as he was beginning to fish his favourite pool where a burn runs into the main river. Here the water rips over a shingle beach to strike into the almost vertical face of a tree clad bank. In the angle so formed the burn flows in and creates a swirling pool. One had only to look at it to know that if there were any salmon up that some of them must have found a resting place here. The pool was an open invitation to an angler, so unlike much of the water where a stranger was in doubt. Yet, obvious as it was, it still retained something of the perversity common to all salmon rivers and salmon pools. It looked as though it should fish best from the far side – from the spit of shingle where the water lapped the white pebbles in a shallow eddy. In fact, it fished from the near side, from beneath the trees under the high bank, where one cast with a short line into the rush of water beneath one's feet.

My host put up his rod as I approached. He eyed me remorsefully. 'I don't think there are many fish about,' he said. 'I've seen nothing.'

I had already tried two of the higher pools, and I also had not seen a fish. We stood and looked into the black water. The level had dropped another six inches during the night. But it was still running high with a noise of watery confusion. Half the shingle beach on the opposite bank was covered, while in an angle of the stone wall beneath our feet a white crown of froth tossed restlessly.

'You try it,' said my host. 'I'll go down and fish the Haugh.'

'No – you try it,' I said.

But he had made up his mind. He turned and left me, and as I stood on the wall I wondered whether I should have insisted. He had given me the best pool on the river. Still in two minds whether I should follow him, the water twenty yards away parted and a salmon showed himself for an instant. The temptation was too great. The fish had risen about six feet out from the top of the concrete wall – the first fish I had seen for a whole year. It was like seeing a friend on the other side of the street in a strange city, and to strangle the desire for its closer acquaintance was more than I could do.

I moved down the stream, and with a short left handed cast put my biggest trout fly over the fish. It was probably too small a lure for the size of the water, but it had no gut loop of doubtful ancestry. Yet even after I had made the cast, I half hoped that the salmon would not take it. I was fishing from almost immediately above where a strike on a short line, combined with a small hook, would almost inevitably snatch the barb out of its mouth. The line was greased, and a big upstream bend swam the fly gently over the place where the salmon had moved. Nothing happened. I tried a second and a third cast, and when both were refused I knew that I should have to risk one of the big flies which my friend had lent me. There was little doubt that the cold spring water needed something bigger than anything I had in my trout box.

So I made the change. I made it three times – but each time without making a cast. The wretched gut eyes of the big flies, rotten with age, snapped as I tested them. Only the fourth and last fly held and only then because I lacked the courage to give it a real pull. This one good fly was a half-molted thunder and lightning, dressed far beyond the bend – a scraggy thing whose profession in another sphere couldn't have been mistaken. I thought that it could hardly hold a fish for five minutes – supposing a fish was fool enough to take it.

Well – a fish was fool enough. It came up the first time, a picture book rise, like a hungry trout. This was no boil, but a jump, with the head breaking the surface first, followed by the whole body. The fly was taken into its mouth in the upward rise, carried with it clear of the water, and then borne downwards into the depths. It is not often that a salmon takes in such a way.

I dropped the point of the rod as the fish came up, but so short was the line that I felt its weight almost before it touched the water again. Not only was the fly rotten, but I reckoned that the salmon was lightly hooked. It is the fish which has had time to turn before the strain is applied, which is hooked in the angle of the jaw – the toughest and best place of all.

How I prayed that the fly would hold! I had been a whole year without a fish – and now had on a beauty with rotten gear. I walked down the wall and got below him. The current was needed as an ally, for this could never be a straight fight between sound tackle and a sound fish. Every advantage had to be snatched. Fortunately the salmon headed upstream and I held him there, working him with a little sideways strain to tire him. After about three minutes I crept up close above him by shortening the line until the gut cast was showing. I wanted to have a look at him. There he was, almost beneath my feet, close into the wall and perhaps a yard beneath the surface. He was hanging in the current swaying gently from side to side, a small fish about eight pounds. I couldn't help thinking what short work I would make of him – if I could trust that eyed loop of gut fly. Then I had an idea – I would try to gaff him where he lay.

Now to gaff a fish with a short-handled gaff three feet under the water is asking for more luck than an angler is usually granted. A smart ghillie with a six foot shaft would have had him out in a trice, but the amateur struggling with his own gaff prefers to see a fish on the surface before he strikes – and many a good fisherman will delay until his victim is on his side.

There was one thing in my favour. The salmon had not yet seen me, nor was he alarmed, or indeed greatly inconvenienced. He was proving the old adage that the less you fight a fish the quieter he lies. He didn't take any notice as I knelt down and lowered the gaff slowly into the water. Inch by inch the steel point crept towards him, while with the other hand I did my best to keep the rod vertical and steady. The hook was within six inches of his side when I realised that the handle was not long enough to make the strike in the belly. Somehow the fish must be persuaded to come up a few inches nearer the surface.

I was now lying down with the vertical rod arm aching beyond belief, and one finger crooked round the line to stop it running. If the fish made a dash at this stage, the fly couldn't possibly hold. This one sided affair now became an endurance test. I daren't with draw the gaff so as to get in another foot of line. The risk of alarming the fish wasn't worth it. A waiting game was better in the belief that the gentle, if steady, strain would eventually bring him just that much nearer the surface and would enable me to get the point of the gaff under him. At one moment I thought the chance was not to come, for with a gentle wriggle he moved a few feet upstream, almost out of sight, and I was compelled to lower the rod to give him line. But I saw him, within a matter of seconds, begin to drift back again, and what filled me with hope was his new position – quite six inches higher. Down he came, down in a slow drift, close in, and by good fortune, he dropped back almost directly over the point of the gaff. I nearly fell into the river as I struck him. It was a clean vertical stroke without ever a doubt about it. Within a split second the fish and I were floundering on our backs on the top of the wall. Within another second we were both well away from the water, with one of us at least breathing easily again. He was a spring salmon, with the small head of his tribe, and sides the colour of newly minted silver. Such little springers are the most lovely of all salmon, and the best eaters. The only blemish was a cruel scar on his side where he had

done battle with the meshes of a net on the sea coast a few days before – a battle from which he had escaped, only to fall to a fly with a rotten gut eye. His weight was seven and a quarter pounds, and when I looked at my watch, I saw that the time from hooking him to landing him had been six minutes. The fly seemed to be none the worse, and with one fish in the bag, I was now ready for another risk at the same odds. I buried the salmon at the foot of a tree under a pile of grass and went back to the top of the wall.

Fishing to the far side of the river with the same left handed cast, and in the same place, I saw the line three minutes later pause in its journey into my own bank. As I have said, I had been fishing with a greased line, but in the recent fracas it had become water logged, and had now sunk; and, as I say, there was a check – a sudden warning that somewhere down there, there was business afoot.

I had been taught to count three before doing anything on these occasions, and this time it seemed an age before I dare allow myself to tighten up. When I did so, it was solid − but solid with the moving weight of another salmon.

Luck, if you like − and a denial too, of one of the laws of fishing, in which I had always believed. In the playing of the first salmon, I had stood high on the wall immediately over this place, had gaffed him within six feet of where this other fish had just taken, and yet I had not, so it seemed, scared him. Undoubtedly there are times when finesse is wasted on the tribe, when to tread softly is a waste of time.

He was a fighter − a fellow who didn't stand well for the bit. A rush across the pool, another downstream, and a third diagonally into the neck of the pool, followed each other in succession. Each time I had to let him go, fearing for the fly. Then he hung in midstream, shaking his head like a dog worrying his master's glove. I eased the strain, for I know of no more dangerous moment when playing either a lightly hooked fish or a fish hooked on doubtful tackle. The jerk, which is a savage thing in the case of a salmon, will snatch the hook through the flesh or break a fine cast.

As soon as the strain was lifted, he went away gently, but over by the shingle he stopped, and heading up the current, began to work back easily into my own bank. In a second I was going to have my first sight of him. I had more than that − for he suddenly turned, swung down below me, gave me a perfect view of his body, and a perfect chance with the gaff. It was a chance I took. I slashed at him across the back, and across my own line, as he swam past a few inches below the surface; and in a shower of silver drops, he came prematurely out of the river to land in a heap on the bank behind me.

And he was a kelt!

There he lay, stabbed in the vitals – and incidentally revealing himself as a 'she' who had done her duty on the redds, splitting her tail in the process. There was no doubt about it – as there never is any doubt about a kelt. The vent expanded as a thumb was run gently down the belly; the gills were pale, and a few maggots clung to them tenaciously. Not that the maggots were conclusive, for a salmon running for a second spawning may carry them in the gills. But the silver of her sides was not the gleaming silver of the first fish, and although she was well mended, she had not that depth of girth and fullness of line which belongs to the unspawned fish.

I have only once caught a salmon over whose condition there ever seemed to be any doubt. It was a baggot taken in the same river a few years previously – an unspawned fish which had made the long run to the headwaters the previous season, and had dropped back without depositing her eggs. She had the shape, but not the true silver of the clean fish, and she was ripe, too ripe for the early months of the year.

So within a quarter of an hour, I had two fish on the bank, and some explaining ahead of me. It seemed poor manners to take your host's pool and a kelt in the same breath. Yet in a normal April, most of the kelts would have been away – and the first fish had seemed a precedent. Who would not have taken that Heaven sent opportunity of whipping the gaff into it as it swam past?

For the third time I moved back to the head of the pool. Was there yet another fish beneath that dark swirl? I was not to have the chance of finding out, for on testing the miracle working fly by the gentlest of tweaks, the gut eye snapped at last. So I went down the river to make peace with my host. He forgave me – and told me that I had had the first fish of the season. Nor did we see another that day.

Twenty four hours later the murk of London was growing like an odious bubble on the skin of the horizon, and a few minutes afterwards I and my salmon and my briefcase – the last two travelling together – were gliding in to a landing. I had brought with me into the city an indefinable tang of the north which had nothing to do with the broad tail protruding from the flap of the leather satchel!

Such expeditions as these had the same effect upon me as the end of a term at school when I travelled north with the thunder of the wheels beating time with breathless expectations. The feeling of being a schoolboy again was recaptured by the sight of the aircraft on the tarmac – a sense of impending freedom which money could not buy.

'Where's the fishing rod today?' asked the officer in charge on the next occasion. He had become accustomed to seeing it among my luggage, regarding me as improperly dressed without it. Sometimes he disapproved, for when I was flying the Fulmar (a Naval fighter of 1940 vintage) there was the problem of stowing it safely. There was a good space in the machine gun wells in each wing, but in shape and size they were ill adapted to fishing rods. The design of naval fighters of those days left much to be desired.

'Where's the rod?'

I tapped my suitcase. It was stowed among shirts and pyjamas – a special rod on this occasion which might have been created for a poacher, but was equally adapted to staff officers who borrowed Fulmars. I had had it made fifteen years before, when a week's tramp over the Northumberland fells promised some trout fishing. Its five short sections made it equally suitable for pushing down the leg of the trousers in times of urgent trouble or placing more respectably in a haversack or suitcase.

Today I was flying to the north west – to a hive of warlike activity planted on a lonely strip of Cumberland coast. I was answering a summons which had nothing to do with trout fishing, but which had mentioned the subject casually and quite irresistibly. It seemed that there were some fish in the local beck, uncooperative fish like those which are often found in the sophisticated parts of the Test.

'They're only small,' a voice had said over the long distance telephone, 'but they've a wonderful flavour…you might find time to slip down in the evening.'

As an adept at slipping down in the evening, the rod was as inevitable as a tooth brush. Both were soon packed into the Fulmar, and while the rigger was busy strapping me in, I sorted out my maps in the correct sequence. The little strip of Cumberland was now only ninety minutes away – about the same distance in time as my London flat. This morning I believed they would be a pleasant interlude – an unrolling of woods and rivers and hills bathed in sunshine. Only the last fifty miles was likely to be troublesome – coastal fog, said the weather report. But when is not some part of a journey across England difficult? The sun seldom shines everywhere, and if the route runs close to Manchester – as it did today – something unpleasant is almost certain.

I took off over the bumpy grass surface of the field, flicked up the undercarriage lever, and watched the green indicator lights replaced by the red.

Now banking sharply, I swung London round my horizon before setting off up the Thames valley.

The journey had begun with startling suddenness. All air

journeys do. In a moment those irritating thoughts about what one has forgotten are violently suppressed by some such sight as a strange town sliding beneath, and the fear that one has lost oneself before one has begun. On a train journey the whole process is more leisurely. Even after the guard has blown his whistle, there is usually time to kiss a favourite niece again. In the same relative period of an air journey, a distance of ten miles has been covered, and before the train has emerged from the tunnel outside the station, the aeroplane is fifty miles on the way. While these considerations did not count on so sunny a morning, in bad weather they are matters of moment.

I flew low – at only five hundred feet. At this height the hills retain their contours, the valleys their depth. The earth spreads outwards in rich perspectives, distant enough to be safe and not so close that people write complaining letters to the papers. At five hundred feet, when the air is calm, England is a lovely view.

I crossed the Chilterns, as deeply wooded as any hills I knew. This morning they looked as though they carried the trees on their backs as a great burden, half resented, but worn as a woman affects a heavy cloak, for its beauty. The Chilterns are not my country. They are too rich, meriting superlatives which make me suspicious of their genuineness. The sandy heaths, the heather, and the too perfect pinewoods of Surrey give me the same feeling. They are so much like the picture postcards of them that they can't be quite true.

Suddenly, beyond the next ridge, I found Oxford flickering over the top of the engine cowling. Oxford – city of dreaming spires someone has called it – looked a heterogeneous huddle of grey roofs which swelled like a growth as I flew towards it at three miles a minute. As there was no hurry (the sun was to be given a chance to burn up the northern fog) I circled the city, noosed the Wren dome of the Bodleian in a tight turn, and pulled up a thousand feet for a wider view. Through the Perspex side panel of the cockpit, now canted inwards as the aircraft heeled over, I let the spires revolve about me. It was lucky that their architects never saw their creations from where I was seeing them now. No building can stand assessment at such an angle. Somehow I had thought that Oxford could never look anything but dreamy and beautiful, but it was as sordid as any town in the black country – perhaps more so, for it lacked the tidy pattern of modern housing estates.

I circled once again, looking closer in an effort to recapture something of the spell which the city had always cast upon me. What I saw was the foreshortened stump of the Martyrs Memorial and a second later a green square in a grey frame – which was the quadrangle of the House. To recite poetry in the precincts of the last seemed as grotesque as to crown the first with a chamber– each fashionable pastimes in days gone by. Was this the Oxford of golden sunlight under whose trees I had gathered conkers as a boy? Was this the city of unfathomable dignity which can persuade a young man that the past, the present, and the future are safe within its walls? It was difficult to correlate the idea with the view I had through the square of Perspex. There was no dodging the trail of the railway lines or the dominance of the gas works, while the pennants which flew from every clothes line made no attempt to disguise the plain facts – that Oxford babies wore nappies and Oxford men (some at least) affected long underpants. Yet still intent on disproving the obvious, I circled for a third time. Now I looked into the field where I had played cricket, holding the insignificant patch of grass in a tighter and tighter turn, clinging to it with my eyes as a drowning man might cling to a fading star. It was no good. The patch failed to impress me as a site worthy of spectacular feats and powerful emotions. Yet it was here that I had lifted a ball over the hedge on to the roof of Timms' boathouse, achieving a pinnacle of greatness which I would never have believed could be toppled so easily.

Poor old Oxford!

I left her behind and headed for Worcester by Charlbury, Chipping Norton and Morton-in-the-Marsh. It was a route which a conscientious secretary to a touring club might have prescribed for a cyclist, and he could have done no better for an airman. However greatly the northerner's spirit may be stirred by the break of the sea on his ironbound cliffs or by the mist on his mountains, the crossing of the Cotswolds cannot (in the sunshine, at least) but quicken his pulse. They are puny hills by all standards, but they live in the break of their earthy rollers on to the green plain as the spirit of England.

Such emotional characterisation will mean nothing to the foreigner, and possibly to the Cockney... unless he happens to fly over their crests on a summer day, or more leisurely pass through them on his feet.

I had last seen Morton in different circumstances. It had emerged out of the clouds as I had dropped earthwards with an engine out of commission. I had been flying the radio beam to London, wrapped in an unending swirl of grey nimbus. The cutting of one of the motors had changed a technically interesting flight by instruments into an urgent crisis demanding a level landing field and a modicum of visibility. As I dropped lower, it was over Morton that the clouds had parted, and it was Morton which had provided that desirable landing field.

On the other side of the hills, at Broadway, the northern shoulder of the high ground falls abruptly into the lush fruit country. The disorderly pattern of the uplands with their woods and fields is suddenly marshalled into the military ranks of well planted orchards. The change is instantaneous, for as the ground falls, its new character is assumed without an area of transition. I flew down what is called the Five Mile Drive, leapt the cliff-like edge of the hills, looked down into the main street of Broadway where the sign of the Lygon Arms was swinging in a gentle breeze, and in a second was on my way to Evesham. I was vaguely conscious that great battles had once been fought on the flats below, and I thought that no better ground could exist for men who had come down from the hills to pattern themselves into the shapes of armies, to move together, and in gentlemanly bloodshed stand up for their principles. Its rippling levels intersected by gentle streams were made for battle and, growing fruit.

Let me make some haste on this journey. The Fulmar was not as slow as these sentences suggest. Worcester, a dozen miles away, was reached and turned in a few moments. The valley of the Severn was unfolded towards its source, wooded, deep meadowed, and fertile to the edges of the industrial belt, where, wisely, it turned westwards and disappeared into Wales. I came into a land of canals with the hills on both sides, receding in a gathering haze of sun-shot smoke. Then as I approached the Warrington gap, little puffy clouds grew up around me like toadstools. I had been expecting them. They gathered closer until there was less and less room to dodge between them, until finally I was forced to dive into the

Lancashire plain beneath a three hundred foot roof of continuous vapour. The bad weather had arrived. Below me were tall electric pylons tracing lines across the flat landscape. The mist hovered about their tops, but never quite came down to them. At the first sign of their eclipse, I should have turned and sought sanctuary at the nearest aerodrome. The day was no longer something to enjoy, the cockpit had ceased to be a room with a view. At the same time, there was plenty for the eyes to do – watching the pylons, the compass, the network of railways for distinctive junctions, and finally checking with feverish haste the shape of the river estuaries – the Rabble and the Wyre – lest I lost them before I had pin-pointed my position. Even then I should have turned back had not two aerodromes lain directly on my route, each of them unrolling their long black runways beneath the belly of the aircraft within seconds of when they were expected.

The weather was rolling in from the sea – from Liverpool Bay to Fleetwood sands. It had that look about it which threatened a more complete blackout of fog to ground level. Nothing can drain the courage of an airman more effectively than such a threat, and my supply was at a low ebb when the Fulmar whipped me out over the glassy waters of Morecombe Bay, where at last I saw ahead a thin bright light along a clearing horizon. Some trick of the wind, or a rise of a degree or two in the temperature was responsible for that luminance, and as I flew towards it, it grew and widened and became, as it were, the exit to a tunnel. I entered the light and blinked in its sudden brilliance, and as I looked round, became aware of the sea and the distant shore around me. It was as though blinkers had been taken from my eyes, for now the hook of Walney Island was as clear ahead as Humphrey Point up the estuary on my starboard hand.

I had passed Warrington, Southport, Preston and Blackpool without seeing them. That awkward belt of weather, fifty miles wide as the 'met man' had predicted, had lain over the Lancashire plain like a blanket, smothering the smoke of its factory chimneys and giving the air space between the clouds and the ground the colour and transparency of dishwater. I was glad to be out of it and to see ten miles ahead the two thousand foot crest of the Black Combe on the southern spur of the Cumberland coast. it marked the end of my journey. But before I came to it, I swung the Fulmar round to take a last look at the mouth of the tunnel from which I had emerged. It appeared innocent enough, for the sun was beating down on the flowery crests of the clouds which had formed it. It would have been easy enough to have flown over the top of them, never leaving the sunshine for the gloom of the overcast. But it might have been unwise, for I had no wireless and previous escapes from disaster had taught me, as they teach every airman, that it is better to fly under the weather when unprovided with instruments for homing.

Less than half an hour later I was standing on the solid floor of a pleasant room, looking through a bay window at a plume of cloud which now flew like a pennant from the peak I had so lately seen from the air. The sun was shining, and the flanks of the mountain were a fresh green in the morning light. Thoughts of the beck which flowed out of its side were already mounting in my head; speculation was already turning from the problems of air navigation to the prospects of an evening rise of the trout.

As I looked through the window, a companion joined me. He was the station doctor whose invitation to fish had originally seduced me. He began to tell me about the beck and about the little river into which it flowed.

'We'll go down there this evening,' he said. 'It might be quite good.'

So as the evening gathered the light into a splash of colour in the west, we set out. We would have fished the main river had not an accident spoiled our chances. The previous year a load of lime to sweeten the fields had been dumped on the bank, and the bank collapsing had precipitated it into the river. Every fish from there to the sea had been killed – a hundred and fifty tons of them, including salmon, sea-trout, eels and flounders. It was a tragedy which nature would put right, but only in her own good time. It was still too early in the year for migratory fish, and of course, the 'brownies' had been wiped out.

A short ride on bicycles brought us through a veil of midges, past the village church, to a gate in a field, and here we dismounted and waded through the lush grass and its evening dew. It wasn't a good night, but it was a pleasant one, particularly because I was able to show my host a trick by which he could catch his breakfast without expending any energy. As he did most of his fishing in the evening after a substantial dinner, it was appreciated.

The need for specialised tactics was obvious at the first pool – announced as being full of trout, but impossible to catch. The tiny water ran out from under a wooden footbridge, and concentrated itself under the near bank which was about two feet high and a dozen yards long, before it petered out at a cattle ford. It was clear, even before my host told me, that the best trout would lie close in under the bank where the water was deeper and swifter, and that at the point where a bush overhung the stream there was probably an extra big trout.

'Go ahead and try it,' said the doctor. But I shook my head. I was so pleased to be in the clean air again that my cup of pleasure was momentarily full – and to sit on the bank while 'Doc' caught the first trout was my set idea of a programme. I wanted, moreover, to see how he was going to tackle it. There was a row of thorn bushes on the far side, so that unless he fished the run which was under his own bank from immediately below, he would have to stand in the middle of the stream and cast in towards it. I guessed he wouldn't do that because he was wearing a clean pair of shoes and a nice line in fancy socks.

As I thought, he stood on a dry stone in the cattle ford and cast directly upstream. The fly alighted immediately above where he was standing, and in the good light it was not only seen by every trout in the pool, but so was the cast and the line to which it was attached.

'It's a hellish place,' said the doctor. 'If it wasn't for the bushes on the other side we might get some fish out of here.'

I sympathised, and when it was obvious that both parties had had enough, we moved on upstream. I forbore telling my host, benefactor, and good friend that it is necessary to sacrifice your dignity, and maybe your trousers as well, on small streams. The most sophisticated members of the whole race live in such waters. But the very next pool demanded plain speech and plain deeds.

Doc said: 'You can't fish here – there's no current, a brilliant light, millions of trees, and any god's number of bushes.'

It sounded so promising that I said I would like to investigate further. He came with me.

The stream had divided and flowed through what appeared to be a deserted garden with old rhododendron bushes clustering the banks beneath a canopy of sycamores and beech. The banks were perhaps six feet high and almost vertical, giving one the impression of an artificial cutting. The water down below was sluggish and clear, but it was also full of small trout.

'Your move,' said the Doc, with undisguised relish.

Now there was nothing to the solution of a problem like this for a free thinker. It was only impossible to the man who had been brought up on broader waters from whose banks the obstructions had been thoughtfully removed. It was certainly true that you couldn't cast, and that even if you had succeeded, your line would have fouled the top of a bush and prevented any second throw. Moreover the water was so still down below that it would have demanded a quality of casting which was beyond the capabilities of either of us.

I gave the doctor my haversack and my money to hold, and lying full length wriggled under the nearest bush, pushing the rod ahead of me. In a moment or two, I realised I was being followed, and looking round saw the shining face of my friend not far behind. I only hoped he wouldn't lose the money.

We broke out of the other side of the bush overhanging the water, and in a moment we were lying side by side with the rod protruding halfway across the stream.

'When you come down in the world like I have,' I said, 'you'll learn that you have to work for your dinner.' 'Breakfast,' he corrected.

We didn't pursue the distinction, for at that moment a fish rose almost immediately below. There were at least half a dozen rising within ten yards on either side, but this one had obviously been sent by Providence. I unhooked the March Brown from the first ring of the rod and preaching up its hackles, let it go and saw it swing out over the stream. The technique was simple, and of course it is known to fishing tramps all the world over. It is merely the process of dipping the fly up and down on the surface of the water. If there is any skill in it – which I don't admit – it is to allow the fly to touch the surface without breaking its skin. In other words, the hackles of the fly are never allowed to get wet, although they touch the water and send out little rings across the smooth surface at each dip. The process is trying on the wrist, but very easy.

As I expected, the trout down below lost its head. Trout often do when they are treated in this way. Provided they don't see you, they make furious grabs at the fly until they finally hook themselves on its barb or prick themselves sufficiently to realise that there is a catch in it. On this occasion the luck was with us, for after a couple of preliminary darts, the fish was firmly hooked, and after a brief interval, more for the sake of form than anything else, was lifted out of the water and swung into the foliage of the rhododendron beside us.

The doctor was delighted, and soon we were penetrating another bush a little higher up. When this, too, had ended in success, I handed over the rod and bade my host take an active part in the proceedings. Long before the evening was over, I had made a convert to this form of the gentle art, and if he doesn't forget the only essential to its prosecution, he is destined to remove a lot more fish from the hitherto neglected places.

Later that evening, we passed the first pool again where the orthodox approach had previously failed. Admittedly it was now so dark that a cast from immediately below could scarcely have mattered – but the doctor was by now an advanced dapper, and insisted on a stomach crawl across the grass to the edge of the stream. Lowering the fly over the top of the bush, he was treated to the most substantial splash of the evening, to be followed immediately by the thrilling sound of the reel running out. The doctor beached the fish ten yards down in the cattle crossing, and displayed a trout of at least six ounces. It was the best fish of the day.

But the cost had not been light. Although I got my money back and my bag, the doctor had succeeded in getting rid of his beautiful box of dry flies during one of his many crawls. He spent a night of remorse before he found it on the edge of the stream the following morning. By lunchtime that day, and twenty four hours after leaving London, I was back where I started.

V

By Air Again

In the days when the flying bombs were over London, an opportunity to spend a few days in the country was always acceptable. Apart from the average fisherman's natural dislike of a big city, the advent of the noisy intruders heightened any natural distaste for the crowded surroundings. An order to visit a west country base, such as I received one day shortly after the 'doodle' campaign opened, was as welcome as a spell of leave. Not only should I sleep that night relieved of the necessity for keeping one ear open, but the chance of a few hours by the river when duty was done were never better. That the weather was unpromising, and that an unpleasant little aeroplane had been set aside for me in which to make the journey were minor considerations. The worst that the combination were likely to do could hardly compare with the discomforts inevitable upon a train journey, or the interrupted sleep equally inevitable if I remained where I was.

Yet it was to prove quite a day – seasoned by incident which at times made London life seem peaceful. It included an imminent prospect of reducing to produce both myself and my aircraft in the mists over Salisbury Plain, and later engendered a naked plunge into a Cornish river to recover a sea-trout at the bottom of one of its pools. Apart from these highlights, there was the nearby explosion which took place as the electric train was taking me out to the aerodrome that morning, and then later there was the more pleasant train which meandered by the side of the Cornish estuary, with a basket of trout on the seat beside me. In fourteen hours I had experienced many of the emotions to which mankind is heir, and then at last found rest and peace in the sight of the sun dropping down into a calm Atlantic like a ball of fire.

When I set off from London a front was lying across southern England, its outward sign a sheet of grey stratus cloud which for several hours had been dropping lower over the roofs of the city. It had descended from perhaps ten to two thousand feet by the time I had climbed up over the Staines Reservoirs and shaped a course for the south west. But for the moment, visibility remained good. The grey bulk of Windsor Castle stood up ruggedly from the river bank eight miles away; the woods to the south of Bracknell were an oasis of olive green under the lowering sky. The Heston gas meter behind me was standing up like a giant's bucket carelessly overturned, and even the Great West road was visible for several miles on its way to Maidenhead. There was nothing to complain about, although the precaution of marking the map in twenty mile intervals and timing the first stretch to get the ground speed was probably wise. Weather forecasters are not often wrong at point blank range.

The trouble began on the fringes of Salisbury Plain about twenty minutes later. At first it was mild trouble, a lowering of the clouds to about a thousand feet and occasional showers in which the visibility was reduced to two or three miles. But the long straight wood by Hamington had turned up, and the Andover aerodrome, and then Boscombe Down unmistakable by the railway. I was some sixty miles on my way, and in sporting parlance I was still strong on the wing, although down to eight hundred feet. Unfortunately, the ground now came up towards me where the southern tip of the Plain thrust its point towards Salisbury. The clouds, too, grouped themselves into close-set showers whose lower edges licked the shoulders of the hills.

I began to dodge in and out of the showers, streaking round the edge of a little storm, flying up the cloud valley between it and the next one, and getting back on to the course as opportunity offered. I came to the railway running up the Wylye valley from Salisbury to Warminster, and here I was in two minds whether to surrender and escape south eastwards or to make another attempt to get over the high ground into the safety of the Stour Valley. I decided on the second course, chiefly because I felt sure that I was about the centre of the front and that the conditions ahead would improve. It was nearly my undoing. In a few moments I was forced into a narrowing gap between the clouds and the rolling downs, and then into the depressions of the downs when their summits were covered. A big wood flashed beneath my wheels, and a quick glance at the map placed it with practical certainty as the one which climbs up the side of the nose dividing the Wylye and the Nadder. There were two hills just under eight hundred feet high on my right. I couldn't see them, but the map had them marked in big type. My altimeter was reading under five hundred feet, and I was only just below cloud level… I could see the smooth grass waves unrolling like an Atlantic swell for a mile ahead and reckoned that the crests of almost any one of them would be good enough for an emergency landing. As they sped close under the wings, the rain came on. It obscured the windscreen (which was already clouded with oil) and almost persuaded me that a discreet landing where I was would pay the best dividend. Then without warning a succession of low huts flashed below, followed by the outline of a picketed aircraft, and finally by the small but glorious sight of a wind sock. I was over an aerodrome, although none was marked on my map. Thankful for the mercy, I didn't stop to reason why, but throttled back, and making the narrowest possible circuit lest I lose it again, found a strip of wire netting and without more ado sat down on it.

It was a relief to feel the jag of the undercarriage as it bumped over the rough ground.

I had landed on an aerodrome without knowing where I was, and I remained in the cockpit in front of the low control building for several minutes, trying to locate it on the map. I was reluctant to ask where I was, but as I twisted round in my seat to survey the lie of the land, the mist came down and blotted out even the trees which I had noted a few moments before beyond the huts. The hills were swallowed by the clouds. There was some excuse, for the aerodrome proved to be new and the area which I had been so diligently scanning on the map contained this field in its centre. I was not five miles off course. The duty pilot was forbearing and confined his comments to issuing an invitation to lunch. Maybe he thought I was tough for having come so far in this weather. Given this chance, I kept the conversation to a gastronomic level and was wafted to the mess and to a lunch which would have cost a day's pay in peace time London.

By early afternoon the front had gone through. The clouds were splitting into individual masses, ragged edged, and blue-grey against brighter patches of light beyond. It was time to go, though sleep would have been pleasant after that lunch. On the aerodrome the raindrops were glistening like a million jewels and portended the sun breaking through before the day was much older. It was so typically English that I didn't notice it. Only Americans from the middle west and soldiers from the east see anything strange about the speed of our weather.

There was a tunnel under the blue-grey clouds. I rushed down it, and came out the other side into a great light which was flooding the plain beyond. All along the horizon there were vertical shafts of sun flinging down pools of gold. on to field and hamlet. Time and space shrank, the engine hummed contentedly, and long before it was time to think of tea, I was circling a Cornish aerodrome in brilliant sunshine.

It was only a couple of hours afterwards that I was breaking through the thickets of a steep valley, down towards a river. I wore a pair of old slacks, and carried a fishing rod. The unpleasantness of the morning was far away, and even the more recent glories of Exmoor and the sweep of the Tavey as I had entered the Cornish peninsula were fading memories. As for my business – it was not scheduled until the following morning.

There is something about a west country valley which marks it out from others. It begins with a silver-tongued estuary which at high tide looks big enough to anchor a battle fleet. But the pretentious beginnings soon dwindle, and in a few miles the mighty anchorage has shrunk to a precipitous little valley choked with vegetation. From the air it looks like a dark coloured snake which twists across the quartered fields. From the ground it is like a jungle hung with

trailing creepers and barbed with a quality of brambles which have no peer. The riot of vegetation is a shock to a tidy mind and I could not help wondering why it is that man should have been so diligent about his fields on either hand and yet have left these gutters to nature.

The river was perhaps ten yards across, although here and there it broadened out into wider shallows. Mostly it was slow and deep, the pools no more than holes. Standing beside one of them, one looked up through a roof of entwined branches which receded higher and higher as the trees climbed the hillside. A more exhausting river to fish would be difficult to imagine. In the space of an hour I had fought my way through a dozen tangles to catch a glimpse of the dark water. I had seen the brown trout feeding in the pools, and by pushing the rod through the branches had, here and there, got a fly over them and had actually caught one or two.

It was difficult to believe that this was a river teeming with salmon during the spring and that at this moment it held hundreds of seatrout. It was difficult to believe that through this half choked channel the tide would come seeping in an hour or so driven up the estuary to invade what looked like a stream many miles from the sea. I only learnt these things from a man who was standing on a little footbridge, a knowledgeable looking man with a rod and a creel by his side. He said some other things which surprised me. He claimed that he had had an eighteen pound fish out of the river within a dozen yards of where we were standing. I looked down into a few feet of open water. A fallen tree was lying halfway across it, while from the opposite side a bush hung over the remaining channel. It was hard to guess where the fish must have been lying, and quite impossible to understand how he could have got it out of such a place.

'There's a deep hole under the bush,' he said. 'More than likely there's a fish there now.'

He read the doubts in my face and launched into a stout defence of the qualities of his little river. It was one of the best salmon waters in the west, while if I cared to come back that very night, he would personally guarantee me a catch of half a dozen sea-trout. 'And there's plenty of small brown trout if you want to fish now,' he added.

I said that I would much sooner see him catch a fish himself, or at any rate show me how he would cast over that impossible pool below us. The tackle which was propped against the bridge was a clumsy spinning outfit, and to use it in such a confined space would have been beyond my ingenuity.

He answered me with a grave smile and proceeded to lower himself cautiously down the bank to the water's edge.

'If it's as good as you say it is,' I called after him, 'why don't you get the banks cleared and give yourself a chance?'

'We like it the way it is,' he answered.

A few minutes later a remarkable thing happened. He foul-hooked a salmon in the hole beneath the bush. He had cast his minnow clear of the fallen tree – a mere lob, but an accurate one. Then he had waited a moment while it sank out of sight before he gently reeled it towards him. It came across the current, guided into the hole about which we had been talking, and here it had suddenly checked as though caught in a sunken root. The fisherman evidently thought that just this had happened, for I saw him jerk his rod back as though in an effort to break it free. When it was followed by a terrific boil in the water I think he was as surprised as I. It was a nice reward for a good piece of casting, but hardly expected.

The salmon went off downstream after showing no more than his side. It carried the line under the bush where it sizzled in its branches, and then suddenly out of sight we heard a heavy splash as the fish jumped. I ran off the bridge, slithered down the bank, and was after it myself in great excitement. More bushes, a clump of flesh tearing brambles, and a ditch were taken after the manner of a tank, and I came up with the quarry in the next pool. I saw him almost on the surface under the boughs of a big overhanging ash, and through the sherry coloured water the bright gleam of the Devon minnow showed clear behind the dorsal fin. It looked like a salmon of eight or nine pounds and from the flash of silver on his side I judged him to be straight out of the sea.

'He's still on,' I shouted, and from upstream came a smothered voice which appeared to be abusing some unseen third party. I left the salmon and ran back, across the ditch, through the brambles again, and came upon the fisherman working anxiously with his line among the tangles of the original bush. It was well and truly fast, with a turn of the line round a supple twig and some sort of a half hitch which had locked it tight. I thought I could get into the river, float down under the bush, and with an upward thrust probably reach the tangle and break it clear. But my companion wouldn't hear of it. He sent me off downstream again to see if the salmon was still on, while he worked out his problem alone. If I had known then that I was in any case to bathe that evening, I should have disregarded his advice, and I believe that between us we might then have had the fish safely out of the water. As it was, I found no sign of the fish down below, and no sign of the line to which it ought to have been attached. So I returned to my companion. We finally gave up trying to disentangle the bush and, instead, recovered the free part of the line downstream by fishing for it under water with the point of my own rod. It seemed to come in quite freely, but when my companion got hold of it and began to hand line it in, there was a sudden and violent check followed by yet another mighty commotion twenty yards through the undergrowth. I saw the line snatched tight and fall slack again. The fish had gone. We sat on the bank, still shocked with the suddenness of it all. It seemed that in the last few minutes we had met more improbabilities than might ordinarily be expected in a day's fishing.

The line was finally cleared by working it from both sides of the bush at once and then the minnow was once again dug into the cork handle of his rod. It had a tiny piece of flesh and a few scales impaled upon one of its barbs.

'It's like that sometimes,' said my companion, 'especially with a foul-hooked fish.'

'You must lose most of the salmon you hook,' I said. 'Now if you only cleared the banks of the stream...'

'It's not really necessary,' he butted in. 'There's a technique to it... If you hold the fish on heavy tackle it's only rarely that they can get out of the pool... I've killed a salmon here in three minutes.'

I looked at him wonderingly.

'It goes against the grain at first,' he added. 'But it's the best way... Look at this stiff rod... It'll stop the biggest fish the river holds...'

It was a new form of heresy, for I had been brought up to understand that a minute for every pound weight was a reasonable allowance for playing time. Admittedly I had bettered it, but three minutes for a fresh run fish...

It was time that I did some fishing myself, and in a few minutes I dived into the undergrowth like a native returning to his forest, and disappeared from the sight of my late companion for ever. For half a mile I pushed downstream through the thickets and then began to fish every little pool on my own account. With only a trout rod and a cast of small sea-trout flies I neither expected nor hoped to hook a salmon. As a matter of fact, a pair of brown trout were caught by clapping from an overhanging bank, and then three more came from a couple of stickles where the river was broad and shallow and there was a clear enough space to make a normal cast. The biggest of them weighed barely a quarter of a pound. It was then that I found a larger pool, closely girt by a riot of low bushes on the further bank, but offering a chance of covering its water through a narrow gap in a similar wall of verdure on my own side. I sat down and was making up my mind where fish were likely to lie when, far down the pool, a sea-trout jumped. It was perhaps twenty yards from where I sat, and just within reach. I decided to go for it from where I was – an easy matter with a greased line. Only the flies would sink, and there would be no sodden line to lift off the slack water. This technique makes stream fishing so much easier that I wonder all fishermen do not adopt it. With the last yard or two of the line left ungreased, the flies swim deep enough for ordinary purposes.

The rod arched under the strain of the cast and the flies shot out in a line to fall some ten feet ahead of where the fish had jumped. There was no chance of laying those smooth curves of line over the still water, which would have prevented the flies from dragging. It was all I could do to make the distance. So to look after the drag I shook a few feet of line from the top joint of the rod and waited, watching the quiet current drifting them down the stream as they slowly sank.

The trout took one of the flies perfectly. It was a picture book example of what ought to happen but rarely does. I saw the passage of the line nearest the fish stop, waited a moment, and then tightened up. In another second I was playing as fine a sea-trout as I had hooked for many a day. For a full minute he raced up and down the quiet pool, and I was sure that I should be able to tail him within the next minute. But the luck which had stood me so well that day departed, and I was left suddenly with a rigid line leading down into the central depths of the pool. It was solid in some snag of which there had been no previous sign. I had let the line fall slack as the fish came towards me, and it had made good use of an opportunity.

I put the rod down on the bank and took off my trousers. I was convinced that this was the last sea-trout I was likely to hook, and it wasn't going to escape for want of a little moral courage on my part. By wading in, I got to within about eight feet of it before the water came over my thighs. So my pants came off, and I got a couple of feet closer. This was still no good, so my shirt followed my pants, and I slid naked beneath the water. There was a steep shelf, and up ending myself I followed it down while it grew darker and darker and the pressure increased on my ears. The pool was of an astonishing depth for a small river. The first attempt brought no results, but at the second I found the cast, ran my hand down it, got the dropper fly stuck into my palm, yet succeeded in freeing the lower end. It had been wrapped round what I took to be a piece of rotten wood – probably an old bit of fencing. Alas, there was no fish. The bottom six inches of the cast was missing.

I shot to the surface, swam back to the bank, and pulling myself out, sat on a grassy patch to dry. As I sat there I suddenly noticed something queer about the pool. The water had begun to flow the other way. The tide was coming in... and I am certain now that the fish had sensed it, become excited, jumped, and taken my fly for no other reason. I have noticed this happen in many rivers, and sometimes with a similar suddenness as the tide begins to leave a pool. I was ruminating on the possibility, when there was a girlish giggle and a scurry of feet behind me. I looked round, saw nothing, but snatched my shirt where it hung on a bramble. One of us was blushing.

I should have liked to have returned to the pool after dark and collected the half dozen sea-trout which my late friend had guaranteed. But courage broke down in the face of the ten mile walk down the nearby railway track after the last train had gone. Time was in any case short, for in a few hours I was due back in London, and in a few more I had to be in the north of Scotland. So I put up my rod and scrambled up the hillside to where the single track cut a path through the jungle. Half a mile away was the wooden platform of a little halt, and as I came to it the smell of creosote combined subtly with the scents of the trees and the smell of the wet earth. After a while an absurd little train chugged round the bend and pulled up with important snorts. The sporting side of the visit was over.

On the following evening, I was once again contemplating a forest, but this time a forest of chimneypots from the windows of my high perched London flat. Thoughts of the new journey were already in my mind, exciting thoughts about a strip of northern coast, which was an old favourite. I was taking the road to Dornoch, the long road which runs as straight as a die across the border until the hills take you into their arms and the breath of the heather is in your nostrils. I should be there soon after lunch, and if work was to keep me busy throughout the rest of the day, the night was to be my own. It would be a night quite an hour shorter than it was here in London, but amid what surroundings! Those acres of grey roofs over which I was looking made me feel almost unreal with their picture in my mind.

It was not many hours afterwards that I saw the gleam of the Northumberland sands beneath me. The weather was clear and sunny, and I was flying a fast American passenger aircraft. It was good to flash over Berwick and look down again on Scotland. There was the iron bound hoof of St. Abb's Head, and away in the distance the gleam of the Forth. I flew on over the Bass Rock and out over the firth, with May Island to starboard, and then I was over Fife. In a flight of ten minutes across the water I had short circuited a journey which took two hours by train. I whipped into a steep bank over Loch Leven and noosed it in a quick circuit, looking down at the boats making the familiar drift along Mary's Island, and searching their passengers to see whether one of them had a fish on. But they were inactive, plying patiently at their rods, and I turned north again to fly down the Tay, cutting across the top of Budden Ness where I had so often waited for geese, and then turned up the coast for Aberdeen.

The air now had the crystal quality so seldom found in England. It was the quality which on past occasions had enabled me to see the peaks of the Grampians from a hundred miles out over the North Sea, a snow blink in the winter months with the hilltops hard against its background.

There was no need of a map as I flew north. I knew every headland, every stream, every village. The tide was rushing into the basin at Montrose, pushing back the waters of the South Esk. It had already filled the Long Shot, and by the dwindling stream which flows into the boat pool I could see that it was attacking the straight which leads to the bridge. If I could be down there with a rod in the next few minutes, I reckoned that the chances of getting a sea-trout would be good. I wondered how the old bailiff was... I could see the red roof of his cottage and the glint of his bedroom window where I had left him a year ago with heart trouble.

Now the cliff which overhangs a fine pool of the North Esk was catching the sunlight. It shone like the polished face of a panel of Australian redwood, and it brought other memories flowing back of the slippery stance at its foot and of the autumn salmon which had risen, torpedo – like, from beneath the ledge. Then the cliff and the pool were gone, and there were the familiar ghosts of other waters. -the sea pool at Inverbervie and then – after a jump across the purpling Braes of Glenbervie, the noble valley of the Dee. I found myself looking away from the city of Aberdeen towards the hills, westward, to the cradles of Banchory, Ballater and Braemar, hills dark with the cloak of rich timber, the river showing as an occasional silver splash... all this crowned by the blue peaks of Carnferg, Lochnagar and Ben Avon. One day I would fish this Dee... one day, fish the best of it. It was a promise of long standing, but not despaired of. I was still thinking of it when the village of Alford on the Don was suddenly below. It was a bend in the river which reminded me of the strange individual whom a friend and I had christened the 'melancholy man'.

It is queer how the buzz of an aeroplane engine will divorce one's mind from the present and encourage it to wander unchecked through the years. The 'melancholy man' went out to this bit of river below each morning, carrying a nineteen foot pole and an expression on his face which wasn't an inch shorter. At six o'clock he came back, following the long course of the river from the lower pools, and still carrying his gigantic rod at the trail. In the hotel he sat at a table by himself. He never spoke, never smiled, and wore clothes as sombre as his face – tweeds without a pattern and a cap without a character.

For a week he went out in the morning and returned in the

evening, and he never got a fish. Then on the last day I saw his figure from afar coming up the bank. As usual he was returning from the lower end of the beat, and the measure of his melancholy stride was as constant as the swing of a pendulum. But today there was something strange about him. He was carrying something in his left hand. I put down my rod and waited. As he drew closer I saw that he carried an enormous salmon secured head and tail by a cord, its body bent into an arch by its own weight. It must have weighed thirty pounds. On he came, head sunk on to his chest and the tip of his rod bobbing in front of him like the antennae of an insect. I coughed, but he passed within a yard without raising his head. No chance to congratulate him, to ask him where he got it and how. He was as remote as a mountain. He went on towards the hotel, and soon afterwards I followed him and made inquiries about the weight of his magnificent fish. But he had gone, dissolved almost like a spirit manifestation. They said that he had wrapped up his fish in grass and paper, and with the parcel under one arm, had walked out between the gates to the station without saying a word.

'A quiet gentleman,' said the hostess. 'But such a gentleman.' He had left a £10 note for distribution to the staff.

After leaving the Don, I turned north west, and climbing, made through scattered cumuli until I came out over their tops at seven thousand feet. From here they looked like dabs of cotton wool on a patchwork quilt. Such clouds give one a sense of speed at a great height. They come rushing towards the aircraft, and to leap over their turrets and minarets, or to dive through their arches, is as exhilarating as hedge hopping ten feet from the ground.

From here, I could see the bold outlines of Peterhead through a wide gap to the north east, and in the north the mountains of Sutherland were a broken line of purple. Ahead, through another gap in the cloud, lay the silver tongue of the Moray Firth. Now I had glimpses of the Spey almost immediately below; of the Findhorn basin looking no larger than a duck pond, and the forest of Darnaway no bigger than a cabbage patch.

This is a country of great rivers and great fish. Not one of them bears a name which in many an angler's mind does not rouse some vivid memory of his sport. Don, Ythan, Ugie, Deveron, Spey, Findhorn, Nairn. I crossed them all, and then turned outwards across the Moray Firth for the Black Isle and Cromarty. Through some trick of the light the mountains were a blue-black and the lochs a dull silver. Here and there on their sides was a splash of light where some burn cascaded over the lip of a fall. Down below the heather reached almost to the sea, and the marshes flickered in deep yellows and dark greens. I had seen the light strike on the rivers Alness and Glass as I passed, and now losing height I swept into the Dornoch Firth towards the hungry mouth of the Carron, the Shin, Oykell and Cassily. These are rivers with a temper. They foamed whitely over their rocks and had no lowland pastures where they were tamed before emptying into the sea loch.

I have seen Arctic seals chasing the salmon almost into the fresh water, and on the heights above them I have tried to stalk wild cats. These places do not belong to man, even though man has set up his crofts amongst them. They will be among the last to be tamed by advancing civilisation.

Less than four hours out of London, I closed the throttle of my aircraft and heard the rush of the wings through the air as I drifted to a landing. Yes – there are good aerodromes up here, scratched out of the thin soil of the coastal fringe, but still broad enough for anything which flies. As the propeller gave its last kick, silence took the place of noise, and then out of it came the cry of a sea-bird, and slowly as my ears grew accustomed to the quiet, the tinkle of running water.

That night at dusk I was many miles away with a long standing companion whose genius had organised the transport and the authority to be where we were – beside the waters of a remote loch. We had taken a chance, gambling on the warm evening bringing up the brown trout for a night rise. It was a water I already knew and loved, and returning to it was like meeting a long missed face. In the gathering twilight the well remembered features were withdrawing one by one. By Shark Point the water was already as black as ink under the pines, and there was a merging of the shadows under the opposite shore. Here on our own shore we had built a fire, and this had already begun to throw a light of its own. The handle of the cooking pot was glowing like a hot poker in its reflection. Beyond the circle of the firelight the track by which we had come was almost lost in the darkness.

My friend Peter sat on his haunches, listening. 'It ought to happen soon,' he said.

I stopped sucking at my pipe and listened too. Yes, it certainly ought to happen; but there was no sign of it yet.

In a minute a grouse called, and then faintly from down the track came a clear shrill squeal. But round about us there was nothing. Even the voice of the water which would usually suck at the peat under the bank was silent. There was no ripple and no breath on either the water or the sides of the hills. There was only colour – the last pastel tinted wash of the sunset as it drained out of the sky. It was surrendering now to a growing host of stars.

We got up and stretched our legs, breathing in the warm heather scented air. I looked across the loch, and saw the mirror like surface, thick as quicksilver. I could make out the irregular smudges of grey stones on the far bank, the ruins of some croft a relic of lichen crusted blocks which are the memorial of a hill people whose tide has ebbed. No sound, no movement, no breath came from the hills.

'Yes, it's bound to come soon,' I repeated.

Peter folded the cloth with which he had been wiping the pan and stuffed it into a pocket of his haversack. The haversack held our rations, cooking pot, oilskins, fishing tackle, and rubber fish bag. He stood up, and moved towards the boat. 'Let's push out.'

The ripples sped away from the stem as he stepped on to the floor boards. The splash of the water could have been heard a mile away, a sudden savage explosion of the silence. I followed and with a thrust of the oar we slipped into the bay. There we sat on the thwarts, waiting. Conditions were perfect and the quiet of the day didn't make me believe any less in the certainty of fish tonight. A high temperature, a wind from the west south west, and the month of July were surely too strong a combination. So we lay there and waited, and at a few minutes after one o'clock, a wraith grew up on the water as though the loch had suddenly breathed. In ten minutes a mist had spread from shore to shore.

'I still think they'll rise,' said Peter – and he filled his pipe, suggesting that he was prepared to wait until dawn. And then, as though his determination had in some way communicated itself to the trout which had been lying invisible, the surface of the steaming water was broken.

First a single plop, then two more, and at last like a summer rainstorm, a hurricane of rising fish. The mist was still lying about us, but now it stirred, parting here and there on a breathless wind of its own making. The dark surface opened up into a score of concentric rings and in the west there was still sufficient light to catch the glint of the ripples.

I saw one big trout cruising on the surface with half its back out of the water, its dorsal fin like a sail and its mouth open like a scoop. It had happened all in a moment, but not before my line was shooting towards the cruising fish. A Coachman fell in front of it, and was taken while it still floated. The leisurely cruise was interrupted, and changed into a fight for life. A moment later Peter's voice came out of the darkness, speaking to himself. 'Got you, my lad…' and there was a commotion off the stern of the boat and then silence, save for the retch of a reel as the fish won a yard or two of line. A puff of wet air came from behind us and a wave of vapour rolled over the boat and passed again. My fish was now beneath me and I was afraid of it working under the keel or becoming entangled in the reeds which lay in patches over the bay. The strain I was putting on it would have almost stopped a grilse. The trout was just coming up as a flash of light from the other end of the boat showed Peter's forearm with the landing net sliding forwards in a swift, sure, action at which Peter was an expert.

'You ready?' came Peter's voice – and the torch flashed again. It caught my fish in its circle and without further word the net slid out once more and returned. Peter had big hands and he could grip the torch and the landing net in his grasp and operate both with fascinating precision.

'Nice fish,' he said. 'A pound and a quarter – mine's not such a good one.' But I had seen the glint of his torch along its side as it lay curved in the net, and I knew it was as good a fish as mine.

The character of the loch had changed. I doubt whether ten minutes had gone by from the time we were sitting waiting for something to happen, and having the first two fish in the boat. Now as we disentangled the fish from the cast and the cast from the strings of weed clinging darkly around it, we listened to the music of splashing trout. It was a continuous sound – though how long it would last was in the lap of the gods. Trout don't lose their heads like this for long, and the moment was an opportunity for speed, accuracy, and ruthless tactics.

Peter was using his rod like an elongation of his arm. He was always free from worry about timing and direction. Had he been blindfolded, he could have hooked and landed his fish with the same speed and certainty, for like a good hunter, he was able to substitute ears for eyes, and he had a knowledge of his tools which needed no visual check to ensure that they were being properly used.

Good friends who are good fishermen, have so often refused to go with me on night ventures upon summer waters, for no other reason than that they are unsure of themselves. They have not practised casting with their eyes shut or learnt to know by the weight of the line how far away their flies will fall. They are dissuaded by memories of entanglement in the opposite banks of swift rivers or chaos in a boat on placid lochs.

I think that we had both learnt the grimmer lessons of night fishing. We had, for instance, our spare casts ready soaked – powerful 1x gut which we would have discarded in low water as too heavy for the summer salmon in the river not twenty miles away. If we had a tangle, the cast came off and a new one was tied on. And we brooked no knots that meant a savage hack with a penknife in the dark, preferring the simple hitch which anyone can untie blindfolded in less than two seconds. We had two flies on each cast big flies with fine sharp barbs. Peter was using a Number 8 Grouse and Claret, and a Butcher, while a Coachman and a big Greenwell were on my own cast. On the spare cast there were two other big flies I think that one of them was a Peter Ross. It didn't matter, for when the fish come up on a fine night, they have no discrimination. Yet just in case of a trout proving particular, I had half a dozen one and a half inch Demons dressed with Peacock spears and Golden Pheasant crests on Number 10 hooks – a lure which will tempt almost any trout that ever rose in a hill loch on a summer night.

So we fished hard and fast as the last light drained out of the sky and the mist hovered like a doubtful ghost. We lay in the bay thirty yards offshore, and for fifty minutes of excitement we never moved. There is no need to move on such occasions. The fish cruise about the surface, many of them with their dorsal fins out of the water, and come one after the other to the angler.

All that was heard was the splash of the trout and the hiss of our short lines – lines nine or ten feet long at the most. The technique was a slow trailing of the flies through the water with the rod describing an arc either to right or left, sweeping the stern or the bows, and maybe after half a dozen casts a quick pluck, and an even quicker flick of the wrist. Half the trout were only pricked – and that is the way with trout at night. They take the fly well enough, but the angler doesn't know it. The only warning he gets is the pull, by which time the fish has either got rid of the fly and the angler remains in ignorance of it having ever been taken, or the barb snicks through the lip in the lightest of holds.

We had seven fish in the boat when Peter hooked his big one.

He struck it as though he were delivering an upper cut – and afterwards he said he had been watching it for some minutes and knew what he was up against. Only his phenomenal night-sight could have made such observation possible. I stopped fishing as Peter's line came across my own.

'I'll try not to be long,' he said. 'But for the moment he's top dog.'

The reel was retching as the line was pulled off. I could vaguely see the white plume where it cut the water close to the boat. And then the retching turned to a scream – the line was torn off the drum with a sound that every fisherman associates with a big sea-trout or even a salmon foul-hooked. I got out the oars and rowed after it without comment.

'Funny thing,' said Peter. 'I couldn't stop it.'

The fish had bored deep. It was in the reeds. We rowed right up to it and now the line fell slack on the surface. We unshipped an oar and stirred slowly. The water was blue-black and it was a matter of feeling gently to free the tangled forest from its roots. Maybe the work took five minutes. Neither of us spoke, but as a big weight down below came away and gradually rose towards the surface, Peter turned on his torch. A mass of dark green ribbons came into view with no sign of the trout. I swore, but Peter stepped across the thwarts, and, asking me to balance the boat, hung himself over the side and began to part the floating weed with his hands. He had flung several pounds of it dripping on to the floor boards when he made a sudden wriggle inboard and snatched his rod. Simultaneously I grabbed the net, but in the darkness I couldn't see anything.

Immediately under the gunwale there was a splash, and before either of us knew what was happening, the line was streaking across the loch and the reel was humming. It was then that Peter permitted himself the observation that it was a grand fish. It was and for another full minute we fought it on the surface in the way we would have fought a salmon which was determined to break out of a pool.

Then gradually he brought it in. This time I was going to make no mistake with the net, and as the fish came in towards us, I had torch and net ready.

'All right – let's have some light,' said Peter.

Aiming at a point five or six yards out on the quarter, I switched on the light. It caught in its circle a sudden seething commotion of black water, and out of the middle of it came a trout – head,

shoulders, body and tail a foot clear of the water in a shining, dripping arc. I had never seen such a trout. It seemed to hang suspended in space for us to see its lines – the depth of its body, the dignity of its small head, the marking of its sides. Half drowned, fought to a standstill, it had yet flung itself clear of the loch in a last fury of despair.

It fell back with a noise that could have been heard a mile away.

I stood up, keeping the torch on the spot, ready for the net. Within a matter of seconds the record for the loch was going to be put out of reach for ever.

'All right – relax,' said Peter.

The tone of his voice was unmistakable, and I almost knew what I should see when I swung the torch round on him. He was fumbling for matches in his pocket, the rod resting slackly against the thwart.

'All over,' he said gently. 'I wasn't ready for that jump.'

I switched off the light and we sat wrapped in the velvet blackness. The scratch of a match and a little splutter of flame lit up Peter's face for a moment. His hand was steady above the black pipe hanging out of the corner of his mouth. The lines of his face were gentle – his expression contented. But I myself trembled with frustration.

Presently we both grew aware of a change which had stolen over the loch. It was quiet again, and the gleam of the stars was brighter. In the new and startling silence we realised that the rise was over. As dramatically as it had begun, it had finished. Peter wound in his line – he had not bothered to look at it until now. Eighteen inches of gut were missing from the bottom of the cast, its end curled into a little corkscrew suggesting how great was the power which must have been applied to break it.

Within a few moments and without further word, Peter picked up the oars and drove the boat through the weed beds to its moorings. An hour later we dropped down the mountain side, digging our heels into the spongy peat and looking up now and then to see the sky flushing in the east.

The first grouse had made his morning call, the pigeons were stirring in the wood lower down the slope, and beyond it, in the valley where a pasture reached up to the hill and a stream tumbled over its rocky bed, I heard the voice of a wild duck. In a few minutes a new day would be upon us and the night would seem far behind. Already I was thinking of my flight back to London, of the prospects of the weather, and the chances of being in time for lunch at my club.

VI

First Salmon

In the blood of most of us there is a love of mountains, and sooner or later it is likely to translate itself into a long and possibly uncomfortable pilgrimage so that the heart's desire may be satisfied. Thereafter anything may happen. A man may develop a notion for imperilling himself on vertical rocks, or less dangerously satisfy mysterious longings by climbing to cool summits by gentle paths, or even find his consummation in looking up at the peaks from the valleys. I find myself a member of the last class, but not before terror had driven me from the rock faces of the Lake District – particulary from a crag in Borrowdale from where a friend had dangled me on the end of a rope. But still a worshipper of high places, another friend who returned from Skye, told me about the black skyline of the Cuillins, of the serrated battlements swept by silver mists, of rivers dashing seawards like earthbound storms, and finally of sea-trout to be caught after the rains. Nothing would satisfy me until I had seen them with my own eyes.

Today I should have taken an aeroplane and made the journey with speed and comfort. But only the most enterprising of my generation had at that time appreciated the possibilities of the air. The first Gypsy Moth had just blossomed as the private owner's answer to a prayer, and I had actually committed myself to making a circuit of an aerodrome in one of the earliest models. But that I should fly as far as Skye, never, for a moment, entered my head. So it was that I made my way laboriously northwards in a battered, but conscientious motorcar… a piece of fortune which, as it turned out, introduced me for the first time to salmon fishing.

We had come to Invergarry at the end of a long day and decided that we could go no further. The road ahead through the glen was rumoured to be atrocious. Ten miles on it climbed the back of a barren highland where a lodging would have been out of the question. At Invergarry there was accommodation.

After the car had been put away and its owners refuelled, they found themselves with a perfect evening at their disposal, and decided to walk to the river for the pleasure of looking at the water. It was chance that brought them to the salmon leap where one of the dramas of nature is played out every season – whenever the river is at a suitable level.

At this point the combined waters, gathered from the peaks for thirty miles to the west, are constricted into a defile. It is so narrow in one place that it looks as though it could be jumped. The defile is known as the Falls of Garry and at its western entrance it is guarded by outcrops of rock through which the weight of the lochs, rivers and burns, from the ultimate slopes of Sgurr a'Mhaoraich which guard Kinloch Hourn in the west, concentrate into the bottleneck. It is this neck which forms the final obstacle – a torrent of water pounding downwards for perhaps a hundred yards before it empties into a turbulent pool below.

We stood on a little footbridge spanning the gorge. There were trees all round us, but upstream they parted and showed the level reaches of a narrow loch. The peace of that motionless water was almost unreal beside the maelstrom of the roaring falls. We looked down into the water below, expecting nothing, save the fascination of the racing river. But as we looked a shadow flickered below the surface, moving against the rush.

'It's a fish,' I shouted. But in the noise my companion couldn't hear me. He was pointing down into the gorge again, and following him I saw another shadow flicker through the storm. Our eyes followed it until it came to a shelf of rock running out into the

stream, and as it fought its way onwards a wall of water descended from above and caught it off its guard. It was lifted like a feather and dumped on to the shelf. As the water receded it lay and dripped the silver liquid from its deep flanks. For perhaps a second it was knocked out. Then it curved its great body and its tail smacked the flat rock to lift it high. In a moment it was back in the river, hanging just below the shelf, motionless, as though its utmost strength and speed only just matched the current. This was the truth, for as we watched a wave again came down from above and the salmon had not the strength to meet it. The water took hold of it like a stick, bore it broadsides, and rolled it over and over downstream. The rate of its descent was sensational, a revelation of the speed of the water. The last we saw of it was the gleam of its side as it was flung back into the cauldron below.

The salmon were running. The lower pool was boiling with their impatient bodies. As we stood there, fish after fish fought its way up towards us. Some failed to get as far as the bridge, but one or two reached the shelf where the first salmon was beached. There was one salmon, a big fish of probably thirty pounds, which reached the final waterspout beyond which the level loch spread peacefully and unruffled to the west. It had been struck against the rock shelf, but had recovered and with a magnificent spurt had reached the temporary shelter of a cliff face on the opposite side. From here it had finally made a lunge towards the last obstacle, to climb its solid trunk of water, to tremble in the very breach where another yard meant safety and peace, only to fail, to be carried back, and rolled helpless at increasing speed through the hundred yards of boiling water to the pool from which it came. Not a fish succeeded in running the falls that night.

Up till that moment I had never caught a salmon. But from then onwards I determined to let no opportunity go by without trying. These were surely the strongest and gamest fish in the world. To pit strength and wits against even the smallest of them on light tackle and in moving water must surely be sport worth waiting for. I had seen salmon caught before, and had made a cast or two over rising fish while angling for trout. But the trouble and patience required for the hooking of them had never seemed quite worthwhile until I saw for myself the measure of their qualities as I stood on the bridge over the falls of Garry. Since then much water has flowed under that bridge, and years afterwards I was able to fish this very river, from its headwaters where the River Quoich gulched from the mountains, through the narrows of Loch Quoich, and down the Garry as far as the Kingie Pool. Admiration has not grown any less with familiarity. Every hard fought battle has increased it, and when one is finally lucky enough to see a graceful body lying on the shingle at one's feet, its side perhaps scored by the marks of a coastal net, or its back bearing the scar of an encounter with a seal, or more recently with an otter, and one realises that at last this struggle to reach the headwaters to spawn has ended, one feels proud to have tried one's skill against such an adversary. Today I never take that highroad over to the Isles without remembering this first chance visit, and the sport and the expense, and the hard labour it eventually enjoined.

For weeks I have gone down almost daily to some river and cast out a lure in the belief that finally the luck would change. When pools had been combed and hope of catching a fish abandoned, I have crept inch by inch along the banks, peering into the water, on the chance of at least seeing what I had been unable to take.

Sooner or later a dark shadow would present itself beside a rock, or suspended like a thin cloud above a cirrus of shingle, and gradually knowledge had come about the lies, and because of it I would begin to catch an occasional fish. I learnt the hard way on – small rivers where salmon are few and where, for reasons best known to providence, lures or baits usually excite no interest. It was such a hard way that had not the grip of the sport been so strong, a logical person would have given it up. But like a keeper I know on a famous river who scorned the free feeding trout for the infinitely difficult salmon, I also surrendered to the lure of the bigger game. And as is certain to happen one day, there came a moment when a pool was crowded with fish and when each and every one of them seemed to hurl them selves at the fisherman's bait. The reward was complete, loyalty to a mistress justified.

By five o'clock there were nine salmon on the grass between us. 'We ought to have our photographs taken,' said Joe. I thought about his suggestion, but then in my mind's eye a picture sprang up of similar photographs in the sporting journals, usually featuring a greater number of salmon and garnished with stouter gentlemen than ourselves, and with ghillies leaning on gaffs in support of their knobbly knees. I don't think we would have made as good a picture.

It was, of course, a great day. The fish which now lay on the grass represented an afternoon's work in a big pool on a small river. All of them had been caught on a golden sprat. It was the sort of success which has had the result of convincing an angler new to salmon fishing that a sprat is the best bait – in fact that no one in his right senses would use anything else. The disillusion which is liable to follow leads from bad to worse – to similar baits, graduating from Devon minnows to articulated plugs of an ingenuity rarely seen outside a pedlar's tray, and finally to new and miracle working reels complete with books of instruction ten pages long. That so much can be started by a golden sprat and a day when the salmon come for it like a pack of starving wolves is often an unsuspected misfortune. Yet today there had been no doubt of the efficacy of the flickering gold shadow. As much might, of course, have been done with a fly, but somehow one had had the feeling that a strong arm, a lump of lead, a wire trace, and the little gold fish out of a bottle were, for all their crudity, the talisman by which miracles were to be accomplished.

There had been a flood. A four day spate in mid September had held the river at a sufficiently high level, for a sufficient time, to admit the autumn run of salmon. It had reached the precise place where Joe and I had arrived with our spinning rods. The fish had halted, baulked as the river had begun to fall, by a difficult weir, and crowding the big pool which lay a quarter of a mile below. Neither Joe nor I had caught anything the first time over, although we had seen plenty of salmon jumping in the soupy water. As was to be expected, they were showing in places where they would never be found in low water – far down the flat where the stones could usually be counted on the bottom. A stretch of water three hundred yards long had become a contiguous pool, from the old run in over the heavy boulders with their umbrella of mighty trees, to the broken weir and the little island at the bottom. What had been a glancing cascade emptying into a pot, was now a turgid highroad of water, moving at a relentless pace.

Joe said that the fish were running, and the porpoise-like leap of a cock fish within a few yards of where we stood made it only too evident. There's a forward urge about the leap of a running salmon which is not often to be mistaken.

'There's more than enough water,' said Joe.

We walked up the bank again towards the head of the pool – not so far as the run in, for this was an unfishable torrent now – but to the pot below it. I lay down on my stomach and leaned out over the earth bank. The river was within two feet of the top, but what led me with hope was the twig I had pressed into the clay at water level an hour before. It was two or three inches clear of the surface.

'I believe we'll get a fish yet,' I said to Joe.

The flood had certainly turned, and there had been no more rain since the previous evening. The water was dirty – you couldn't see the flicker of the sprat thirty inches beneath the surface – but there was the chance that the newly dropping level would change the mood of every salmon in the river. It might have been worth while swimming a bunch of worms close in to the bank where many fish would undoubtedly be sheltering out of the main stream. But the sprats were all we had, and worms meant a mile walk to the farm across the fields. On the other hand, each of us had the sort of tackle which was needed on a water like this. Joe was using an ancient Nottingham reel with a twenty pound line, while I had an old Falloch of enormous dimensions, furnished with a dressed casting line and a lighter backing which must have given me a total length of at least a hundred and fifty yards. My rod was short and stiff – an unresponsive pole which could have probably lifted a dead weight of nearly ten pounds. This was not a day for the finesse of thread lines and fixed spool reels. To use such equipment would have been as absurd as going after elephant with a pea shooter.

Today every fish had to be held against a mighty head of water, and there was no following a rush downstream. Tall bushes stood at intervals along the bank.

'I'll fish behind you,' said Joe. 'Get yourself down the river and don't fall in.'

There was a sparkle in his voice as though he knew that something was going to happen. And it was no disadvantage to fish behind another man today. The water was at that height when a row of anglers twenty yards apart would have made no difference to the individual chances.

I flung my sprat far out into the flood, let it drift and sink, spinning slowly towards my own bank. The current of this usually quiet stretch was now heavy enough to bring the lure to the side without winding in. Recovery was effected afterwards, where I specially hoped for a strike. Nothing happened.

But up above, Joe let out a yell as I was making my third or fourth cast. He had hooked a fish. I put up my own rod and went to watch him. A few minutes later I gaffed a salmon, which he had handled with merciless efficiency. He proved the old saying that attack is the best method of defence. I doubt whether he was five minutes over it, which was not long for a fifteen pounder fresh up from the sea. That fish would have taken thirty minutes to land on a thread line and a light rod, and a quarter of an hour if Joe had not been on top of it from the start.

Before long I was into a fish myself, and he was soon shaking his head like a terrier shakes a rat. But I had just seen Joe deal with similar tactics, and I had caught his enthusiasm and optimism for furious sport. I held on, and in six minutes a twelve pounder was grassed.

It would be more in keeping with modesty to draw a veil over the proceedings of the next two hours. An account of slaughter may even now give the impression that salmon fishing is a series of furious battles the day long. It was certainly true that any novice could not help catching them – a point which struck me forcibly as a salmon came up and took the sprat under the bank as I was about to lift it out of the water. Whether the bait was cast into the middle of the river or just dangled at the edge, there were salmon waiting for it.

The best fish of the afternoon was one of twenty-five pounds which Joe landed in ten minutes. It was the last fish of the day, and by that time we had nine on the bank. Our arms were so tired that we decided to stop.

Comparing notes afterwards, it was interesting to find that my companion had landed five, lost three and had renewed his sprat four times, while I had lost two and had made six changes of bait. The losses were perhaps unusually low for spinning – no doubt due to the avidity of the fish and the large single triangles we were using.

We were able to return to the river on the following morning, when we found another rod already on the water. He had done nothing. During the day four rods, including ourselves, fished it, and the result was two fish. The opportunity had come and gone. During the eighteen hours we had been away, the water had dropped another foot and was now no more than a few inches above its summer level. The whole of the lower end of the pool was not worth fishing, and of the two fish which were caught, one was taken in the run which had been unfishable the previous day. It was now possible to wade the upper part of the pool, and those salmon which were showing had left the sides of the river and had concentrated in the pot and the channel leading out of it. Standing thigh deep in the water it was possible to see one's boots. Thus do the conditions of the smaller rivers change in a short time.

A dozen times in as many years, friends have asked in semi-confidential whispers: 'Where can I get some good salmon fishing?'

I remember one friend in particular – a self-made and wealthy man – who put the question, and the answer in his case was simple. I told him to ring up the nearest Sporting Estate Agent and to ask what he had on the Wye, Tweed, Tay, Tummel, Dee or Spey. In other cases the answer has not been so easy. It depended upon what the angler had to spend, whether his desire was to catch fish, or just to fish, and finally on the time at his disposal.

I suppose that the safest approach to salmon fishing is the first way – by one of the famous rivers. Its disadvantage is the enormous sum of money required for a month's sport at the best time of the year. On the other hand, the tenant does catch salmon, and if he is rich enough, the price is worth it. The sequel to my friend's question was that he took the advice and had the kindness to ask me to fish his beat. When he arrived on this water, tulips were in bud, the trees had a cloak of fresh green about them, and there was the blue haze over the mountains which was the first sign of approaching summer. In another six weeks or so the river would be dead, but before that time there was a substantial part of the spring run to go through.

The keeper called at the house on the first morning to show him the river… initially on a handsomely engraved map, and then in person with a proper armament for angling. A month later it was all over, and by that time the tenant had had his money's worth and reckoned that he was a good salmon fisherman. I don't know the total number of fish caught, but it was nearly a hundred, and it included some big ones of over thirty pounds. After the catch had been sold – or as much of it as remained after many fine fish had been dispatched to friends less fortunate he could not have been greatly out of pocket. Indeed, I overheard him mentioning to a fellow member of his club some months later that salmon fishing is not so expensive as unknowledgeable people believe… not to real fishermen.

But I was never quite convinced that the fishing of which he became possessed rightly fell within the category of angling. The river was a lovely river and flows through some of the grandest mountains in the world. Its pools are wide and generous and its salmon fight for dear life as they do in other rivers – and their average weight is so high that fish for fish the sport is greater. On the other hand, its organisation caters principally for stout men who are not happy when taking exercise. The only man who works is the ghillie who rows the boat... and he doesn't mind, because his employer, if he is the right sort, will make it one of the highest paid rowing jobs in the world.

You can fish the river with a fly, and many people do. But the big golden sprat is perhaps the only reasonable bait in the early part of the year, and it lingers on until the fishing deteriorates in midsummer. It is the manner of working the sprat which had never appealed to me. To sit in the stem of a boat with two rods lying over the stem while the ghillie, with great skill, works the ship from side to side, dropping ever downstream, savours too much of mackerel fishing with a hand line.

Most of us are destined to begin on leaner waters. In so many respects it is better thus: better for the soul as well as the purse. But whether you are rich and go for the big river, or poor and perforce direct yourself to lesser waters, there are still decisions to be made. Are you going to be one whose pride and delight are boxes of gleaming minnows and whose reels are so delicately perfect that their proper place is with the family heirlooms, or are you going to be a salmon fisherman in the old fashioned sense of the word—which means the possession of a serviceable casting rod and a box of flies? You can, of course, be both, and if you intend to open your apprenticeship in the early spring when the water is still cold, it will be as well to possess spinning tackle. There are ways too, of working a prawn during the summer months which may make the tackle a thing of price.

I am not going to try to answer my own questions, but mention of them has conjured up a picture of a beach and a narrow channel of water twenty yards wide where I rose my first salmon with a floating line. It was a May day of cloud and sunshine, fresh with the scents of recent rain which had turned the river to the colour of pale sherry. I had hung my fishing bag on a branch of a stunted tree by the bank, and had walked out across the shingle to the water's edge when I saw the salmon rise. It was a head and tail affair which only showed his dorsal fin above the water, so quick that one was inclined to rub one's eyes and ask whether one had really seen it. For the first time my line was greased, and on the end of a fine cast was a small Blue Charm so lightly dressed that I should have once thought it to be useless.

It was a good salmon lie, although the backwater at my feet made it clear that the line would be awkward to manage. All I knew about greased line fishing was the necessity for letting the fly swim naturally and slowly with the current, moving gently across the river as it went. Drag was to be avoided; so was speed. Hence it seemed sense to throw a loop of the line downstream so that it would keep up with the fast current at the far side. I was using a stiff sea-trout rod that day, because my ordinary salmon line looked too heavy for this delicate technique.

It was an easy cast, and I managed to get the fly within a foot of an old post that stuck out of the water at the far side. But the subsequent behaviour of the fly was alarming. It skated over the surface and passed above the fish like a seaplane trying to take off. A second attempt had all the appearance of being a complete bungle. The line was draped in curves right across the river and the fly was at least a yard short. On the other hand, the fly didn't drag, and a gentle sweep with the rod laid the line nearest to me downstream. The next few seconds were among the most thrilling I have ever had. Like a slow motion picture, I saw the salmon come up and roll over the place where my fly ought to have been a few inches below the surface. I waited, but nothing further happened until the fly was more than halfway across the river. And then the fish again surfaced like an old porpoise, rolled over the fly and was gone again. It had followed the lure the whole way across.

I didn't catch that salmon, but I rose him twice more. And later in the day I rose two more and hooked a fourth. Although I lost the fish, I had had the fascination of seeing the whole thing developing under my eyes, and I decided there and then that I would henceforth try to learn something about greased line fishing and to use the method whenever the conditions were possible.

It was a good decision, not only because I believe I have caught more salmon than I would otherwise have done, but because I have had so much pleasure out of it. Like dry fly fishing for trout, you can see the fish you miss, and on a day when the bag is still empty when you go home, this is a compensation. After fishing a river all day with a deeply sunk fly, it is so easy to believe that there are no salmon in the river – although half a dozen may have followed your fly without you being aware of it.

It was a fetish at one time to make a mystery of greased line salmon fishing, as it was for trout thirty years ago. The truth is that it is neither difficult nor mysterious, and that a man who is incapable of throwing a straight line can practise his incompetence to his heart's content with every advantage.

I think that if I was never again allowed to fish this method for salmon that I should make little effort to obtain sport. It is a sentiment of which I would have been hard to convince that day so long since above the falls of Garry. But when secondary rivers only are available, and those often in the public places, a man demands something more than the mere exercise of casting. It seems important, in fact, to advance the art of salmon fishing nearer to the art of trouting with a dry fly – a metamorphosis more nearly accomplished with a greased line than in any other way. Then to the pleasure of angling is added the pleasure of finding the fish and planning an approach. I find that I can enjoy myself for a long time beside a river without catching anything in this way. But to fish one of these reluctant little rivers with a deeply sunk lure in the hope that one day a salmon will catch hold of it is no longer the pleasure it used to be. To float a fly gently over a salmon which has been carefully stalked, to see its reactions in the clear water, and quite often to rise it, is almost recompense for failing to do anything more. And then finally when a fish is hooked, the lighter tackle and the singlehanded rod which blend so well with the method show a quality of sport which has no equal.

VII

The Laird and his People

When I first went to the Highlands I didn't understand the people. They spoke so little that they gave the impression of being jealous of their thoughts. It made one feel an intruder who was unworthy to be admitted into the privacy of the highland mind. I thought myself to be a cosmopolitan and well travelled. But it seemed that I was not good enough to trade in the open market of their ideas. Who were these dour people, unsmiling, with their economy of words that they should refuse me intimacy? Were they not a race who lived in crofts, or bleak stone houses set amongst treeless landscapes, without the amenities of life and largely without its culture?

How stupid the misunderstanding was! And yet it still exists like a barrier made of some gossamer material of strange and immense strength. But now I understand it better, and whenever I am admitted into the circle of the people who live in the north I feel proud and honoured.

My friend 'Mac' is a laird. But basically he is no different from his shepherd. In appearance both are lanky skeletons from whose shoulders rough tweeds seem to droop. They have the lean and hungry look of a Cassius, are wrapped in an aggressive sort of silence, and to the southerner seem unfriendly. I remember being struck by the difference between Mac and his shepherd and a party of English people who were staying at his house. The English, I amongst them, wanted to see the sun rise from the top of the mountain which was across his valley. Mac had deputed his shepherd to act as guide, and then at the last moment decided that he would come with us. We made our way in the darkness among the boulders, a long climb, until we stood on the peak waiting for the sun to lift himself over the ramparts of the opposing hills. There were exclamations of delight, not unmerited, for the scene was one of grandeur before which English tongues are apt to be loosened. But I was watching Mac and the shepherd. Mac, who was leaning on his stick, his body a figure of sharp angles, his face as grave as a stone image, was looking with the rest of us towards the east. Never a word passed his lips, never a flicker of enthusiasm for the prospect which was unfolding. The shepherd seemed equally indifferent.

One of the girls turned to Mac and said excitedly, 'Isn't it wonderful... the most marvellous sunrise ever... go on, Mac, say something.' And I remember Mac answering in his dry voice without turning his head. 'It'll be raining before eleven o'clock.'

It was not until a long time afterwards that I realised that Mac was as deeply impressed as any of the English on the mountain top. But with him it was an emotion that was in the marrow of his bones, requiring no expression or sudden quickening of the pulse to enjoy. He was more a part of the hill top, more a communicant at the altar than any of his visitors. This is perhaps the mystery of the highlander.

One day, years after our first meeting, it fell to the shepherd to take me to the loch where the local river had its birth. We were to have a day after the trout and the shepherd was to act as ghillie. It had been an even slower process getting to know the old man than it had his master. Mac had lost a little of the highland remoteness at his lowland school; he had contacts in England and was even, upon occasion, to be seen in London. But the servant was a virgin gem, uncut, unpolished, as he had risen from the barren earth sixty years before.

But by now I was getting to know him better, and on this particular day he talked.

'There are not many young men about these glens,' I said. 'Where do they all go?'

'To the toons,' said the shepherd in his noncommittal tones.

Then added as a gesture, 'There's nothing for them here.'

So it was that I came to ask him whether he had a family of his own, and learnt that he had one son who thirty years ago had taken the road to Glasgow and the sea.

The fish were not rising, and I pursued the subject. 'Is he still at sea?' I asked.

'Aye,' replied old Andrew.

'What branch of sea faring?' I inquired. 'Did he go in for the engine room or the deck?'

'He went in for the deck,' said Andrew, and then after a pause: 'He's the captain of the Carpathia the now.'

So Andrew the shepherd had a son who was the captain of an Atlantic liner, and if the son had been a judge of the supreme court or a cabinet minister or merely a millionaire it would no more have been cause for surprise to his father, or ever a reason for him changing his manner of living. Andrew was a shepherd, the boy Jock was a liner captain. No doubt there was the same singleness of purpose which made each a master of his profession. There was no incongruity or sense of embarrassment when the liner captain made his occasional visits to his father's cottage. There was no sense of inequality between them, no surprise or enquiring of the mind which could ever sow seeds of unrest. This is the way of the highlander.

Mac had his square stone dwelling on a road which ran deviously round the coast and then after many miles debauched into a small fishing port and market centre. It was a road which skirted sea lochs, twisted, turned back on itself, ran straight for a mile or two beside tide washed rocks, and then plunged inland across boulder strewn mountains, to finish as it began, as an afterthought to a main highway. Instead of being an approach to a house in which lived a civilised man, it might have been a track by which lost highland souls trekked into eternity. Close beside it the laird had his house, and a dozen of the few trees which grew to a height of twenty feet in the neighbourhood. They were strange looking trees, bent to the eternal wind, and on a winter night they made a moaning which required all the warm glow of a fire to tame.

It was the trees that I saw first when I rounded a bend in the valley. They were a break on the naked slope which caught the eye and held it; and then as the dark roofs grew out amongst them it seemed more than ever that this must be a wayside halt on the road to perdition. What strange sights and sounds were not to be seen and heard in their precincts?

Yet as I drew closer, I saw that the house had a white painted iron gate like a lowland villa, and a show of slithering gravel which curved up to the square door, and that on the south wall was a stretch of hot house glass with some blood red flowers behind the panes, proving that, after all, the wild was held in check. I could see as I dragged at the iron bell handle that the trees broke on this side, and that between the hills was the glitter of the sea.

'So this is where Mac lives,' was my first thought, and it was half with foreboding and half excitement that I tugged at the bell a second time.

Then suddenly he was there himself, standing framed in the doorway. His sandy red head and the bush of sandy moustache stood on the stem of a long neck, and the neck in turn was the extension of a body as thin and yet as straight as a good tree. Seeing him there, so grave and remote, I wondered why it was that highlanders grow long and thin. It was easier to understand why they were silent for after time enough in the company of sheep, it is thoughts which fill a man's mind more readily than words his mouth. Mac's people came from the Isles, but a kinsman had left him this fastness on the main land. Because he was quiet in spirit and strong in the arm, and be cause he was a great fisherman, and a little because deep down in his soul he was a poetic highlander, he came here to work. In a modern age he cared for none of the wonders belonging to it.

It was only during the first few moments that the house had seemed depressing... the glimpse of the square, stone flagged hall with the silver topped daggers pinned to the naked wall, and a worn rug before a closed door, the head of a stag, and a brass urn without a plant in it, a rack of sticks, and a deer stalker on a peg with a pepper and salt Ulster... the bleak trappings of a house without a heart. But, as I say, only for a moment. As I entered the room on the upper floor I knew that I should come here again and again and discover more of those things which had lain round the corner of an Englishman's understanding.

As Mac opened the door he was saying: 'You must have had more than enough... what was it? Three hundred miles? And mostly bad road... ah, here's tea... come in, man...'

And I found myself in a room as square as the house itself. The first thing that caught the eye was the red flicker of the fire dancing on the silver furnishings of the tea tray. Around the fire was a steel fender with a leather topped seat – an upholstered fence for the open grate. And everywhere, save for the easy chairs and – of all things – the quarter size billiard table in the middle of the room with a gigantic oil lamp standing upon it, were books and more books... piles of them in friendly disorder.

I noticed other things too... the rod case in the corner, the ancient typewriter like a bishop's throne on a desk piled with papers, the wild fowling prints on the wall between two of the bookcases, and lastly the pewter on the stone over mantel and a collection of oddments from pipe cleaners to school photographs.

Mac had surrounded himself with defences against the loneliness of all that lay beyond the windows. He lived here with a man and his wife to run the house. Inside the house were his strong points. Outside were the sheep... many hundreds of sheep and a tract of rolling highland which, in winter at least, must have demanded every ounce of his physical stamina.

I was to see Auch-na-Rhuie in the winter, once to help dig out more than a hundred ewes from a snowdrift under the Long Wall, more often to go with its owner in the short twilight down to the estuary after wild-fowl. But even Mac was occasionally driven into retreat... to Edinburgh, or sometimes to London, where his striking leanness, red hair, and penetrating blue eyes, to say nothing of his clothes, made him an arresting figure.

'It's early yet for the loch,' Mac said, 'but there are a few sea-trout in the river and one or two salmon in the lower pools.'

I nodded contentedly, chiefly because instinct told me that I should catch fish here.

'Are you busy?' I asked.

He smiled an enigmatical smile which might have meant anything and said that he had inoculated three hundred ewes that day, as well as caught a sea-trout for our supper.

The river was a short one, little more than twenty miles from the source to the sea. From the ridge behind the house, you had the lie of it below you, and I climbed up here on the next morning, and surveyed it. The sea was open to the north west, a broken coast with smoky islands lying indefinitely on the horizon. As I stood here a grouse called, a flock of curlews moving like a single bird whistled and flickered as shadows against the yellow-green valley below, and immediately above the knoll on my left a hawk was pinned against the sky on motionless wings. Where the hills opened the valley cradled the estuary, holding the river against the far slope where the rocks broke through the skin of the earth. Inland, the silver ribbon twisted and turned, the gleam of its shingle bright in the sunlight. Opposite the house it swung to the far side of the cultivated fields and disappeared three miles away round a bend of the valley, capped here by rolling slopes which were now a rusty brown with the old heather.

Fifteen miles away by the track, a hill loch gave it its birth. It was a fine loch, two miles long, and scattered about it in the wilderness were smaller lochs, some of them little more than tarns, but every one of them holding trout. I was to fish some of them. But it was the estuary which I loved and to which I always returned. It is a grey stain twisting across a green and yellow marsh. There are places in it where the turf floats on an underground sea of brackish water, places which rock under the feet like rotten ice when you walk over them. In the winter there are pools, and the Mallard, Widgeon, Teal, and Golden Eye flight in at dusk. When the moon is up the air is alive with wings far into the night, and at dawn they will flight again from the sea, or from the fields scratched from the shallow earth in the valley.

The sea is a bare half mile away from the rocks which let the river out of the mountains. Between the rocks and the sea is that grey ribbon, swelling and dwindling with each tide – the highroad to immortality for innumerable sea-trout, a few salmon, and occasion ally a silver half breed which seems to be a mixture of a brown trout and a sea-trout. It is, as I say, a grey road – but only in the after light of the northern day and in the false dawn which creeps behind the shoulders of the hills. I have seen it as flaming gold, and then later as melting silver as the sun drops like an ingot into the western ocean. Sometimes when the clouds pile up over the highlands, driven by the hot wet winds of summer to grow into the thunder heads, it is turned into a black snake, ominous and evil.

Across the head of the estuary is the stone road bridge, and immediately below it the first of the tidal pools in which a salmon occasionally – very occasionally – will take a fly or a minnow. Twice a day the current of the pool is reversed, and at spring tides the level of the water rises a full two feet, covering the long tongue of pebbles downstream of the bridge.

Three quarters of a mile lower down the river enters the sea. Between here and the bridge is the marsh, with a few scattered boulders on the firmer ground between the slopes. Black peaty banks and an occasional stunted thorn bush mark the course of the water – a water which grows greener against the hair, weeds waving from every stone as the sea is approached.

Above the flats is to be heard the never ending cry of the birds. It is a wild orchestra without harmony, and yet miraculously without discord. It seeps into the human mind until it becomes a background to life itself – a unity which the fisherman can share. It is only towards dark that the voices quieten, and later, throughout the night, there is little to remind you of the former bedlam. Now a cry is most likely to be the death cry of a bird or beast caught unawares by an enemy. There are foxes in the hills and they come down raiding at night. The high pitched squeal of a rabbit is as common as the call of a feeding duck. It is now that the little sounds of the estuary come into their own – the sucking noises of the tide in the middle reach where the high water laps the feet of the reeds, and the increasing merriment of the shallows as the tide runs back and the impounded stream can sing again. All the water noises return with the dark, and among them is the splash of jumping fish. If a fisherman came here without previous instruction or experience, he might be at a loss to know where to cast his flies. There are flats between the bridge and the sea, unlikely looking places. Yet in each of them where the current is slight and the water about three feet deep, the young sea-trout often lie in dozens. There was a head of them in the river on this, my first visit, and Mac and I went fishing for them the next day. We were within twenty yards of each other, and moving downstream a step at a time. Mac was taking out fish after fish. But I myself never had a touch, although I was fishing in front of my host and had first chance of the water. When I could stand the click of his reel no longer, I walked back and met him as he came out of the river in his streaming waders.

'How do you do it?' I asked.

He swished his rod through the air and stamped his feet, and slipped his creel off his shoulder where it overturned on the sea slimed pebbles to spill nearly a dozen bars of silver – not one of them less than half a pound.

'Can't you catch them?' he said.

Every one of his trout had taken a Maloch's Fancy, and he had been fishing with three of them on a fine cast. He only had one more of the pattern left, and it was soon on the end of my own cast. Within an hour I had seven fish myself, and if the tide had not driven us back and put an end to the fishing, I might have equalled his bag. It was sometimes like that in the tidal pools. They would provide damning evidence that the one pattern theory is not always applicable.

There are tricks about this estuary fishing – and the repertoire varies as between river and river. From minute flies to feathered terrors of brilliant reds and blues, there are a score of lures. Any one of them may work on a particular day – to the exclusion of the others.

On one day Mac would be down on the sea reach casting his long line diagonally across the ruffled flat. With flies sinking deep and rod held motionless, he would be taking fish two feet or three feet under the water. The next day I myself, fishing the middle flat, would be throwing the same minute flies, but instead of diagonally downstream, at right angles to the river, and the fish would be snapping them on the surface almost as the flies landed. On the following day, and maybe for a whole week, they would take no lure of any kind, however it was fished, and then suddenly they would come on again for a well sunk Demon. It was only when the shepherd came down with a fifteen foot fishing pole and small demon-like terrors of bright colours, which he worked in long rushes with the top of his enormous rod, that we were forced to acknowledge that this, after all, must be the right method. But it was only right for the shepherd. When we ordinary mortals tried it, we had no luck.

The salmon seldom took in the tidal water. But in the early months when the weather was dry, the lowest pools became holding pools. To see the salmon jumping in their silvery brilliance was to feel that catching one of them could be little more than a formality. Actually, one never had more than a bare chance. I remember a particular salmon which was a fair example of his brethren. I saw him first as he jumped at the tail of a run. The spray of his fall spattered the water within a foot of my waders.

It was an easy place to fish. The river had straightened out from a right hand bend and the beach on my own side crowded the water under a rough stone wall which had been built to preserve the pool. At the end of the wall the current had bitten out a bay from the earthy bank, leaving a swirling hole and a backwater beyond. The fish was jumping in the swirl. The day looked like being a lucky one, for the conditions of light and temperature were perfect. As my first cast drifted across he came up again, clear of the water by a foot. With a little luck he would have fallen back across the fly and foul hooked himself. I tried him twice more and then again with a bigger fly which was, perhaps, suitable for a colder and bigger water. To accentuate his indifference he jumped again.

I was back in the afternoon with smaller flies. As the tide came into the pool, he became very excited and jumped three times in quick succession. Then as the flood stopped the current, he went down and was not seen again. The following morning I was back once more at the pool, and soon he was showing himself as before. During the ensuing six hours, with proper respites, he refused three varieties of Devon minnow, a sprat, a prawn, and about thirty shillings worth of flies. He even ignored a fly dangled in the current from the opposite bank immediately above him – dangled and allowed to drop back a yard or two before a slow recovery. He jumped right across the cast during this ceremony. Meantime the weather remained warm and dull.

On the third day I caught a small sea-trout on a Mallard Demon at the exact place where the salmon should have taken.

There was a complete change of weather during the ensuing night. The wind went round into the east and blew half a gale with a low temperature and frequent hail storms. Between the storms the sky was a hard light blue and the skyline of hills was cut sharp round the horizon. It was a good example of a cold, highly unstable air mass behind a cold front. One would have said that the chances of getting a fish were particularly slender.

The lowest fishable pool at ten o'clock that morning was the middle reach with the salmon in it, and there, sure enough, he showed himself as usual. I was, however, not to be led astray any more, and continued to fish down the run above him on the chance of a sea-trout. I was certainly not going to change my 3x gut and the small peacock demon I was using for any special attack on such a crafty old enemy. And when a good sea-trout of just under two pounds took the demon off the stone which marked the end of the wall, I was well satisfied. He was the first fish I had had for two days, and only the second in the last three. After an exhilarating fight which took us through the broad pool below the wall and into the flat beyond, I beached him safely on the edge of the pebbly shallows.

Mac arrived on the river at this moment, without a rod, but with a glint in his eye, possibly occasioned by the biting wind. He was looking at my sea-trout when the salmon jumped once again, and without raising his head he said, 'That sounds like a taking fish... have you tried him?' Having done little else for the past three days, my reply must have sounded short, for without saying anything Mac picked up the rod and walked upstream along the strip of beach until he was opposite the tail of the wall. I followed, feeling glad that he should have the weary privilege of casting over the brute.

The tide was now coming into the pool. The run in had lost its rough ripple and in another ten minutes it would be smoothed out into a gentle glide which soon afterwards would reverse its flow. When I came up with him he was running the fine cast through his fingers but he made no comment upon its unsuitability. He swished the rod and spun the line out through its rings until it was singing far out over the water. At last he let it fall about three yards above where I knew the salmon to be and where Mac knew it lay without ever having seen it. I had a sudden premonition that something was going to happen. The line checked, as I knew it would, and waiting a few moments I saw Mac take a couple of steps downstream and tighten up. The strain came on, bending the rod into a steep curve. At the first attempt, he had hooked the fish I had pursued for three days on a trout demon with small hooks and a 3x cast.

Mac showed no surprise. He went to work on the fish with silent determination and got below him where he drowned the line and put more strain on the cast than I would have believed possible without it parting. For a minute his tactics had no effect, but finally the fish turned and made a rush downstream into the broad, shallow flat, now bereft of its current by the rising tide. Mac succeeded in keeping it on the move for fully five minutes, and during this time a hailstorm blew up and drove its icy pellets into our faces so that it was scarcely possible to see where the salmon was playing. He was out in midstream in one of his rushes when I saw the line suddenly go slack. A second afterwards Mac was slowly reeling in. He lifted the last of the line off the water, peering at it through the blinding storm, and as it was whipped above our heads we saw that the cast had parted a few inches above the lure. My host handed me back the rod with one of his rare smiles, apologised, and told me that if I hurried I should probably get another fish in the upper pool. He himself melted into the hailstorm on his way to the hill behind where he had business with the sheep.

A second fish seemed to be the height of improbability. The first was surely no more than a lucky chance in a thousand. But I trudged up to the pool as the storm blew itself out and reached it shortly before the tide had begun its final assault. The remains of the trout cast was taken off and a heavy sea-trout cast substituted. A new storm was coming up and the thick gut could scarcely matter in the midst of the bombardment of hailstones which was to be expected.

Anyway, it was unlikely that another fish would put its nose out of doors in this weather. I tied a Mallard demon dressed on

Number 10 hooks to the end of the cast and got into the head of the pool where salmon sometimes lie. It came on to hail, and after half a dozen casts I had begun to feel that the game wasn't worth the discomfort. A veer in the wind was blasting the hail into my face, making the line unmanageable, and driving me deeper into the water in order to reach the channel. Then as I was recovering the line for a final throw there was a solid check which convinced me that I had snagged the bottom of the river. I was just going to give it a savage and frustrated jerk when the snag came to life and shook its head.

I like that slow shake of the head which a salmon gives as it tries to get rid of the hook. It is the unmistakable sign that you have a salmon and not a sea-trout on the line – the shake of a sea-trout's head is of a quicker tempo. If you master it, you will quickly knock the spirit out of a fish.

I made the kill without a moment's anxiety within five minutes and within twenty yards of the hole on whose edge he had taken the lure. As he came to the gaff in the shallow water the hail eased up, and I had scarcely killed him with my little priest before the cold sun was shining again.

The fish – a springer of seven pounds – was one of the only three salmon which were killed in the sea pools that year.

Years later Mac and I spent a night on this pool which dies hard in my memory. It was late in July, and it had been a dry month with a baking sun, so that even the bog holes had opened into a tracery of cracks. But on that particular day the clouds had mounted above the hills until they had become an overpowering canopy of stained thunder heads which at about three o'clock in the afternoon had burst in a great storm. Even down by the sea the raindrops had fallen as large as marbles – a cool, sweet torrent which was sucked up by the dry ground in a long continuous hiss. But over the hills the storm must have been sensational. Repeatedly the sky was split by flashes of lightning while a purple darkness hung down and made a night of the afternoon.

'That's all going into the loch,' said Mac as he cocked an eye to the east from where we stood in the streaming porch. 'It'll be down here by the late evening.'

And so it turned out; But before then the sky had cleared and a wonderful freshness had descended over the earth. Standing in the garden in the late evening, waiting for the dusk, the gentle sound of running water could be heard on all sides. The gullies in the hills were draining, and on the quiet air the sound of it could be heard far off. It mingled with the occasional bleat of a sheep and the distant murmur of the birds over the cliffs.

At eleven o'clock it was time to go down through the balmy dusk, waders slung over our shoulders, and a nip of something in our flasks against the moment when the dawn mists should strike a chill into the air. It was scarcely dark at midnight – there was still a pale wash left over from the fiery colours in the western sky, and always ahead of us the gnats danced in a cloud against the fading light.

The tide was running out of the top pool and the increased strength of the river noises showed how the volume of water had grown during the last few hours. There was a faint colour to it which had not been there in the morning, and the flat below the salmon hole was a sheet of moving silver without a rise breaking the surface. It was still too early, but a sea-trout ripped through the run and sent a bow wave into the smooth water. After rain it was often possible to see the sea-trout running like this, their dorsal fins breaking the surface as they came up the shallows.

On such a night it was policy on Mac's river to use big flies or perhaps a demon. The patterns didn't matter, for the fish would come as readily to a dark Grouse and Claret as they would to a brilliant Teal and Silver, and if I caught more fish on the darker types it was only because I used them more frequently.

Soon after midnight we waded into the water from the shingle beach to fish down the deeper glide under the opposite bank. There was still a little light in the sky, and it was best to make no disturbance in the flat calm. Later, when the night was all round us, it didn't seem to matter how much splash we made. Long ripples could wash out over the surface to shimmer the reflected stars, and still the trout would keep on coming. But it was nearly an hour before the river awoke, and in the meantime the only sound was the stinging swish of the line as we drove it to the far bank. I thought of changing my flies, but Mac, who was only twenty yards away, called out to leave them as they were. If the fish were going to rise they would rise of their free will, and nothing that we could do would persuade them before their time.

Then just after one o'clock, when there was only the palest smudge of milky white along the horizon and the opposite bank was a line of inky blackness, there was a sudden splash. A sea-trout had jumped behind us in the salmon hole. We fished on, and in a moment there came the quick scutters of moving water denoting fish on the surface. To my surprise one of them came from almost between my legs and made me believe for a second that I had dropped something into the water. Simultaneously, there was a scream from Mac's reel. He was into a sea-trout and it was a big one. I could just see the curve of his rod against the sky, and then a few minutes later I was horrified by the ripples driven from his feet as he waded ashore to land his fish. While I was cursing him under my breath, my own line was snatched out of my fingers as I was recovering the slack. It tightened with a jerk against the check of the reel, and the fish was gone. A few casts later I felt a gentle pluck, but once again there was nothing there when I tightened. Within the next five minutes there was a plucking at the flies at almost every cast, but not a single fish hooked. Meanwhile Mac had landed two more, which from the brief play he allowed them must have been finnock.

I was throwing a long line into the far bank at about thirty degrees to the current, and the trout were laying hold of it as it swung in to my own side. I was frustrated and disappointed that I was missing the rise. Yet this often happens in the estuary. For minutes on end, when the fury of the rise is at its height, it seems impossible to hook a fish securely. Then at last a sea-trout took me with a rush. I had not moved five yards down the bank from the place I had entered the river, but for a moment I feared that I should have to follow this one downstream. At one moment Mac yelled out in the darkness: 'Take the little brute away... it's between my legs.' He splashed the water and the trout shot upstream towards me. This time I held him, and got him into the net without leaving the river. I saw the silver flash of his side close in to me and had the net under him before he could move. It was a dangerous trick, and when I lost another fish a few minutes later while trying to do the same thing, I backed on to the beach on subsequent occasions and used my torch.

By half past two the night had gone so well that a temporary halt was called. We had both been twice out of the river to empty our fishing bags on the shingle and relieve aching shoulders of the weight. Now we counted the spoils, throwing a pool of light on to the scattered host of silver bodies. The sea-trout were laid to one side. There were nine of them, of which the best looked to be about three and a half pounds and the average perhaps one and a half pounds. Of these Mac had contributed six, including the big one. In addition, we had twenty three finnock of between a quarter and three quarters of a pound.

The flasks came out and we toasted each other.

Mac said: 'The fish rise like this sometimes, but I'm damned if I know why.'

'The fresh water has woken them up,' I said.

But Mac wasn't sure. He'd fished under the stars many times after rain, and as often as not he'd had little reward.

'And what's more,' he said, 'the river's still rising.'

But I doubted this. It had reached its peak, I thought, shortly after we had begun to fish. The little river went up and down swiftly, and in a single hour could drop a foot after a high water.

We decided that we had done the top pool sufficient injury for the night. The best fifty yards had been fished twice by each of us, and although we could have probably stood without moving all night and continued to catch trout, it was to be remembered that each finnock killed was a sea-trout less for the future.

So we crossed the road and picked our way in the darkness upstream and beyond the limit of the tidal water. The turf was firmer here, and scrubby tufts of heather reached down to the river, while outcrops of rock broke through the surface.

Half a mile up was a long pool guarded at its upper end by ledges between which the water concentrated in a narrow opening. There was a rock plinth on the far side upon which the Nelson column might have stood, but on our own bank the ground was low and opened up behind us into the lowest of the cultivated fields. The rush of water had carried down a mass of pebbles which had been spread generously over the near side and had formed a tongue of heavy shingle which in high water became an island through the erosion of the land behind. Tonight the beach was only partially cut off, and to it Mac directed me with orders to fish down the glide from the heavy water to the flat at the tail of the beach.

Fortunately I remembered the pool well enough by daylight to recall the distances involved. It is difficult, almost impossible, to do justice to a pool at night if you are meeting it for the first time. It is not even easy to estimate to within a foot or two the length of line which you have out when only its weight on the top of the rod is your measure. Mac I left me here and went on up river to try more difficult places which his cunning and local knowledge made feasible.

It was now after three o'clock and we had perhaps an hour before the dawn would be upon us. The rocks on the opposite bank were no more than darker smudges in a well of blackness, but I cast out towards them, and while I still imagined that I had another yard or two to pull off the reel, the cast was on dry land, wedged between two stones. The cost was more than half the cast and both the flies.

It resulted in a change to a peacock demon on six feet of strong gut which was ready mounted and soaked. As I was tying it on I heard a splash somewhere out in the darkness.

A little more than an hour later a scrunch on the gravel startled me into awareness of the world outside the glide. It was Mac, and in a moment I was realising that it was not only growing light, but that he was speaking to me. The sound of the river, so much greater here than among the tidal pools, had deadened my senses like the motor of an aeroplane on a long flight.

'Have you seen anything?' he asked.

I tipped my bag on to the spit and showed him two sea-trout of noble proportions. The best one, a fish of nearly four pounds, had taken me on a voyage of exploration through the heavy water below. It had been impossible to stop, even on stout tackle, and I had finally beached him between two stones more than fifty yards down.

Mac himself said nothing about his own doings and I deliberately refrained from asking him. But as the light increased, and I gathered up the waders which I had taken off for the mile walk home, I noticed an enormous bulge in his bag. So I went over to it and opened it, and pulled out by the tail a fresh salmon.

'I got him at first light,' he said.

Those were great days in a spacious land. There were so many burns and little lochs to fish as well as the river that it would have taken a lifetime to have learned them all. And a life spent in doing it would not have been so hopelessly wasted. If there would be nothing to show for it which would interest a bank, there were invisible assets – the sort of assets which Mac and his shepherd possessed in profusion, both of them men of no account in the world but each immensely rich in a currency which I was slowly growing to understand. Of course to haunt that estuary for its fish and its wild fowl would have been no credit to a man. But to have grown a part of it with the sheep and the self sacrifice and the endurance they often demanded, scratching a living by worldly standards, would have been to grow rich in a way which was forever safe from bankruptcy.

VIII

The Big River

I could hear the sound of the river from my bedroom window. A hundred yards away the water was crowded by rock walls into a narrow channel where its flow was broken into a pattern of white crested combers. Each cliff and grounded boulder was a sounding box to the falling water so that the addition of it was a pervading roar, like a fleet of distant aircraft. At night it submerged the mind as a drug, drowning even the subconsciousness in the profundity of a dreamless sleep. At night, also, when the moon shone, it seemed to be the embodiment of living music, for the flickering light on the broken water lent the fantasy a substance. It never stopped. Hour after hour, day after day, year after year it went on – a fall of irrepressible power and sound which utterly denied the idea that we live in a transient world. In times of flood it had a deeper note. The trebles of its shingle which altered into the canyon were overwhelmed by the deeper roar of swollen pools; new notes were struck on the sharp edges of the gorge, to be flung and tossed from rock to rock in a cannonade of echoes.

This was the big river.

In the mornings, when I walked down the bank with a fishing rod, I often felt as though I were another Alice who had drunk from the bottle which had made her small. The biggest rod shrank to the size of a hazel switch, while the boulders over which I clambered grew to the stature of fortifications. Sometimes I saw another fisherman. He would appear no bigger than a doll, and the patch of water which he covered no broader than a garden path. Yet coming close, I would see that he was casting a full thirty yards. Such efforts were not merely insignificant, but the laws of chance seemed to preclude the possibility of the angler catching anything. There was so much water which could not possibly be reached. I myself sometimes returned to my room at night, frustrated and disappointed, and only spurred to fresh efforts on the following day because I had learned some trilling fact about the river which, added to other trifling facts, might ultimately lead to the secrets of its salmon lies.

The river dominated its valley. Even the mountains seemed to bow their granite heads to its imperious voice. It dominated, too, the people who lived by its banks. It ran through their thoughts like blood through their veins, so that references to its moods continually crept into their conversation. Most of the people lived by it, some by poaching its salmon, others by protecting the salmon, and quite a few by keeping hotels where visitors could stay and watch it. Everyone knew instinctively that if the river was taken away, the valley would be drained of its human population soon after it was drained of its water. Then all the big houses perched above the banks would draw their blinds forever. The pages of sporting journals published hundreds of miles away would have empty spaces to fill, and even that impersonal body of bureaucracy, the Ministry of Agriculture and Fisheries, would miss it.

The river was big business. It appeared to a newcomer, accustomed to small rivers, as an industrial cartel might appear to a clerk suddenly promoted to its board of directors. He didn't know where or how to begin; although he had entry into its councils, he was dumb, because he felt that if he opened his mouth he would say the wrong thing. In the end, this exaggerated respect for the great river wore off, and there actually came a day of moral victory when I could snap my fingers at it.

The victory was won on a pool of long rushing waters. It was a superb torrent gathering its strength before a rampart of shelving rocks which had parted in their centre as though unable to withstand the pressure from above. But it was not a victory of a single day, or the result of a single effort. Others contributed to it, especially a blue-eyed poacher who demonstrated finally that the water could be tamed and even made to perform tricks – like those of a conjurer who produces rabbits out of a hat, save that these rabbits were all salmon.

The pool had three piers which ran out from the northern bank into the swiftest part of its current. They were built of heavy boulders welded together by concrete. Below the point of each was a powerful deep voiced swirl, at whose edges any ordinary salmon fisherman would have said were good salmon lies. The piers were thirty yards apart, and it seemed a certainty that the ninety yards of water downstream must be productive. That, at any rate, was how I assessed it on my first visit. I was alone, and inevitably I chose the northern bank so that I could fish from these attractive piers. The distant shore with its high tree-lined bank and its quieter shallows, with here and there a back eddy where a rock shelf thrust its snout into the faster water, was attractive to look at – a suitable subject for a camera – but hardly worth serious consideration from a fisherman.

I made the journey between the piers three times, first with a fly and afterwards with a sprat.

I saw nothing and felt nothing. Nor, as I learnt subsequently, had I more than a faint chance of doing anything else. The best lie was on the far edge of the rush immediately out from the top pier, and it was only to be reached satisfactorily from the opposite bank.

How could mortal man know… how could he have guessed that the obvious water was only the camouflage of the river sprites who tormented strangers?

However, I suspected something of it on my second visit, largely because of a boat which was moored to the opposite shore. It seemed to prove that the pool must be worth fishing, and fishing from this boat. As it could not possibly be held where the water was swiftest on the northern side, it followed that the unpromising looking shore opposite must, after all, be the right one. This I eventually put to the test. The little swirl off the top pier was left alone, partly because I was still ignorant of the deadly nature of its amber depths, and partly because I was already rowing like a man in a nightmare against the current.

Trailing over the stern was a sprat on fifteen yards of line, and in the upper part of the pool there was sufficient excitement in keeping the craft under control without adding to it by attempts at navigation. So the deadly spot was passed, but the outer edge of the rush was fished lower down, at first too swiftly, but later, foot by foot, as I was able to check the boat, the spinning sprat swinging from side to side, from the shallows under the trees to edge of the torrent in midstream.

It was at a point thirty yards out from the lower pier that the first blow was struck for victory. The initial move was a leap from the butt of the rod which was nearly jerked out of the boat. This was followed by a dive for the rod on my own part, its recovery, and then the mounting thrill of a fight with a big salmon. I had it my own way until the boat swung round in a half circle, a reminder that I was drifting downstream at an increasing speed, and that long before I could hope to kill the fish the fish would kill me. Down below was a place which would have made even an experienced canoeist hesitate.

I learnt during those few seconds what every ghillie on the river knew from the day he took up his appointment – that if a salmon is hooked while hurling alone, it must not be touched until the boat has been rowed ashore. It was panic rather than prudence that made up my mind. I cast the rod back into the bottom of the boat, jabbed the heel of my shoe on the reel, and headed for safety. There was no doubt, looking back afterwards, that this particular fish was as stupid as I was, for it lay quietly while I made my own escape...

one more proof that a fish from whom pressure is removed ceases to fight.

Yet even now I was still sufficiently unnerved to omit the elementary precaution of securing the boat. I had just tightened up on my salmon, when I saw it begin to drift away. Again I made a dive, and again appeared to save a desperate situation. By this time I was wet from a mixture of river water and perspiration, and it was almost too good to be true to find that on picking up the rod once more that the fish was still secure. The relief had its own reaction, for I now allowed myself to be taken downstream, away from the gaff which was still lying in the bottom of the boat. How I landed the salmon I scarcely know. But victory was clinched some thirty yards away, just above the white crests of a new rapid. I fell across its body in a shallow and somehow bore it ashore.

The spell of the river was broken. The despairing days when it seemed that I should never even find a fish, much less catch one, were over. No doubt in another ten years, had it been possible to return each year to this same stretch, I should have discovered sufficient about its salmon lies, and of their variations with the height of the water, to go immediately to the right places, to cast a lure over each, and to know for a certainty that if I caught nothing that there were no fish to be caught – on that day. As it happened, there was no need to serve this apprenticeship. I was privileged to become an honorary member of the river's directorate from whose well of wisdom much was made plain.

As a small river man, I had not realised that such a body existed. I had received permission to fish, had been given a map reference, and let loose without a guide. But the arrival of the proprietor on the river, and then the friendly sympathy which was extended by a merry-eyed looking ruffian in a public house, and finally an introduction to a grave-faced, horny-handed philosopher who was the head ghillie, changed the complexion of my activities. These three men were the cornerstones upon which the business of the big river was built. They were the brains behind the organisation which yielded between them something like three hundred fish a year out of a stretch of a very few miles. There were other members of the firm – the local police constable for instance – who played smaller roles, but who were yet a part of the organisation. On its outer edges, keeping very quiet about their parts, were several hotel keepers who served fresh salmon for dinner at night. While they were less actively concerned in the business, they took

such a personal interest in its workings, knowing almost as soon as the proprietor knew, the position in the pools in which fish were lying, that they could claim to be shareholders, if not members of the staff.

Of the three principals, the poacher had much to recommend him. He inspired the admiration which few of us can grudge to one who knows his business. He was at the top of his class, and to say this of a man from this part of the country is like saying of a cricketer that he is good enough to play for Yorkshire. He was standing next to me in a bar within sight and sound of the river. The unusual liveliness of a pair of blue eyes which regarded me over the rich amber of a pint of ale first attracted me.

'Had any luck?' asked their owner.

It was the day on which I had first fished the big pool from the piers, and I shook my head.

'There's not many fish in the river,' he remarked.

'How do you account for that?' I said. 'I thought the river was always full of fish in April.'

'It was the ice,' he said laconically.

It was evident that he was not to be moved to further conversation, for he buried his head in his tankard and had to be roused by a suggestion that he might like it refilled.

'I'll take a nip,' he replied.

The bartender shook himself out of a doze and reached for a tumbler into which he poured a double portion of whisky. It seemed that I had invested three shillings and sixpence.

I watched the 'nip' disappear as the blue eyes twinkled even more brilliantly.

'Have another,' I said. The invitation was sponsored by a sense of irritation. After a blank day such as I had endured, it was hard to have an offer of beer so freely translated.

'I'll take half a pint,' said the man with a smile.

My heart warmed to him, and as though it was now admitted that I had paid a fair price for a valuable acquaintanceship, I was freely supplied with information. It appeared that an exceptionally hard January had been followed by very high temperatures, constituting a thaw of almost unprecedented proportions. The ice had moved suddenly out of the river, and down by the mouth, a vast concourse of salmon had moved equally suddenly in the opposite direction. They had apparently been waiting for the ice to clear the river. The results were record hauls in the nets, one station collecting three hundred fish in a single day, and a concerted run of the survivors to the head of the river.

We talked on into the night, and when the bar closed went to stand on a rock overlooking the torrent. It was full moonlight and warm – a spring night of calm in which the hiss of the water was the only sound. I realised what an unusual friend I was making. He knew every boulder and the part it played in sheltering the salmon. In our mind's eye we went over each pool I had fished, and he described within a yard where I should find my chances in tomorrow's height of water. As he talked, it became more and more evident that the ordinary people of the river were not generous with their knowledge. I had talked to the postman who brought the letters, the grocer who had supplied me with matches, and the hotel keeper with my bed, and none of them had vouchsafed a tithe of the information I was now receiving. Yet all of them knew something of what I was hearing. It was just that the river folk are reluctant to part with their knowledge, as though it were the one thing in life they possessed which was not common to other men and that they were jealous of it.

We parted that night without disclosing our personal affairs. I didn't inquire how he had come by his information, and he didn't ask me who I was or from where I came. It was actually a long time before I was able to fit him finally into the pattern which constituted the big river. By then I knew him for what he was – a consummate artist in the taking of fish by any and every method provided it was illegal. It was he to whom the grape vine of the river brought the information that Mr So and So of a certain hotel would be glad of a brace of fish on Friday, and he towards whom the less skilled of his fellow poachers turned when unable to fulfil their contracts. When I knew him very well, he told me a story by way of illustrating how easy fish are to obtain once the technique has been mastered. He described how an old friend had agreed to deliver a few salmon to a particular hotel to help out the proprietor with his Easter catering problems. His friend had already expended about ten pounds of explosive before he called in the e:hrpert and admitted that he had failed.

'You see,' said my acquaintance, 'he had made the mistake that nearly everyone makes when he's not accustomed to explosives... he'd used too much fuse.'

Then he went on to describe how he had been led down to the pool that night and shown the job. It should, in his view, have presented no problem to a man worthy of his calling. It was small and compact, although very deep. The job called for less than a tenth of the fifteen pounds of gelignite which was concealed about his person. 'And I thought it was going to be a difficult proposition,' he murmured. 'Man, it was a case for no more than two wee sticks... one with a fuse of half an inch and the other hardly more.'

It appears that a half inch fuse requires a fair standard of moral courage to ignite, for the delay is a matter of only a second or two. In the hands of my friend, however, the margin was adequate, and the subsequent explosion just beneath the surface accounted for twenty seven salmon.

'I felt ashamed,' was his comment as he concluded the story.

Like most poachers who have employed me as their confessor, the driving power behind his depredations was a love of sport rather than a desire for gain. In this respect he was in the same class as the proprietor and his ghillies. The former sold his surplus fish just as the poacher sold his. But either of them would have felt insulted were it suggested that they went down to the river for profit. There was profit right enough, but it belonged to the spirit. Both men started their sporting lives in the same way – with a trout rod on the banks of a stream. If in one case the rod had cost five guineas, and in the other a few pence, the urge was the same. Success in their

respective spheres blessed each of them, and both grew up to be wise and honourable men in. their own way. The poacher on his first fishing expedition with his bamboo rod and his penny hank of gut caught two trout which weighed three quarters of a pound each, and he lost five others. The proprietor caught three trout – so he told me – and they averaged half a pound. They were taken from waters which were not twenty miles apart – though they were separated by as many years. It seemed strange that I should come to know both anglers well, though neither had ever met the other, or heard more than whispered rumours of each other's works. I, knowing both, felt that I concealed a guilty secret.

The head ghillie, too, was dominated by the same all powerful instincts. Where the proprietor was willing to pay several hundred pounds for his stretch each year and travel over four hundred miles from his London offices half a dozen times each season as the urge became too strong to resist, the head ghillie had dedicated his life – and his health. Were all men in their work as determined to achieve its end, as devoted, untiring, and as enthusiastic, the work of the world would be well done. The catching of salmon was the single purpose of his body and his mind, and if such ambition seems narrow, it is because singleness of purpose is beyond our own achievement. We have perhaps never known the peace of complete simplicity and never, perhaps, developed the wise judgement and the true sense of values which it brings with it. The head ghillie had gaffed many a fish for many a visitor. In wealth and importance he was not to be compared with the men to whom his services were assigned. Yet looking down from the high banks to where he and his gentleman were at their fishing, there often seemed to be no doubt as to which of them was the success in life. Were I in need of a man who was a judge of character, I would take the ghillie for my adviser. He was never wrong about a guest once he had had him out with him on the river. His master might make mistakes – and his master was a great business magnate – but not his ghillie.

One evening the three men of the river were together in the bar of the inn. The poacher stood apart, and in the capacious pocket of his loose mackintosh there was a bulge which was possibly the otter he proposed to use that night. Behind the bar was the keeper of the inn, his eyes roving over his customers, knowing perhaps more about their business than they guessed. The ghillie had nodded to the poacher, and the poacher had allowed a flicker of a smile to pass over his lips. The proprietor had eyes for neither of them. He was having his flask refilled while he described to me the loss of a big fish that afternoon in the Graveyard Pool. He had risen it to a fly – the first which had come to a fly that year – and he went on to tell me that he would break the tradition of the big river by continuing to use a fly and prove that even in these early months it was an alternative to a sprat. Along the length of the bar I saw the poacher's eyes twinkling. He had caught two salmon on the fly the night before – not on a rod, but on one of the ten droppers attached to his otter. For practical purposes the case was already proved. I felt a traitor to both of them, and yet I would have given much to have been able to bring them together for the furtherance of knowledge.

When I came first to the river, I believed that I should have no difficulty in catching large numbers of salmon. Others have come to the rivers of great reputation in the same frame of mind. Yet the big rivers work no better for the casual visitors than the small rivers. Of course, if they wait long enough they will catch fish, and probably many fish. The pools will sooner or later fill up with salmon, and at a particular moment – which may last for days – the salmon will take anything which is offered them. At other times, it is necessary to search every yard of water by hurling a sprat backwards and forwards across the current – the dullest and least enterprising kind of fishing I know. Even then there are days when the salmon will not take. They have seen the lures and ignored them, and though one knows that the pools hold fish, there would seem to be no legal device which can rouse their interest.

At the same time, while salmon may be a perverse and incomprehensible breed of fish, I have sometimes wondered whether there may not be a lure which, if presented in the right way, will not tempt the most indifferent. On those days when fish are taking, the character of salmon may not be the same as their character on other occasions.

A man may show a face to the world which would scarcely be recognised when he was laid low by an attack of gout. At such a moment he might fall for a glass of the choicest liqueur brandy, whereas previously his goodwill could be bought for a pint of beer. I am not suggesting that indifferent salmon should be offered, say, prawns in aspic. On the other hand, it has occurred to me more than once that a different approach might be worth trying.

One morning, I was lying full length on an overhanging ledge of the big river watching another fisherman slowly work down the pool towards me. The moment was a fascinating one, for immediately below were two fish, lying side by side, about four feet below the surface. I had already proved that as far as I was concerned it was a day on which they were not to be caught. It may have been too bright, or the water too low, or the air too cold... it was difficult to tell. I had taken fish from this particular pool under what had appeared to be identical conditions. All I knew now was that I should not repeat the success today.

But I watched closely. I saw my fellow angler's fly swing in towards the bank, dropping lower and lower with each cast he made.

It looked most attractive – like a firefly darting through the water. In another couple of casts it was predestined to swing immediately across the two salmon. After passing them it would hang for a moment in the current directly under my eyes, and it was during the ensuing second, when the angler would begin to recover his line, that I felt that one of the fish might strike. But before the fatal cast was made, when the track of the lure was still several feet above the nearest fish at its nearest point, both salmon slipped away like thieves in the night. They had been motionless for the past quarter of an hour. But now they slid gently into midstream where they were lost to sight. Either the angler who was at least fifteen yards upstream, or his lure had disturbed them.

Under apparently identical circumstances on another occasion, as I have recorded elsewhere, I had the good luck to hook two salmon within a quarter of an hour of each other. The second fish had enjoyed the best possible view of my efforts to kill the first, and yet he was not dissuaded from rising to the same lure within a yard of where I had stood.

From the top of the rock, about ten minutes after my fellow angler had departed, I saw the salmon return to their lie. For the sake of the advancement of knowledge, if not for the sake of a fish, I decided I would try to gaff one of them. First, I cut a length of willow from a nearby tree and so extended the length of my gaff to about eight feet. The commission of the crime should then have been simple, and as the iron was lowered inch by inch into the water I felt that the life of the nearest salmon was to be measured by moments. But no! When the hook was still more than a foot from its side, it moved unhurriedly into midstream, and its fellow followed it. There were indeed grounds for believing that these particular salmon on this particular day were more sensitive to interference than they would be when they were in a taking mood. It was as though their wits had been sharpened and that the vaguest out lines of an angler's form seen through the water, or the slowest movement of the murderer's weapon – to which they would normally be insensitive – gave them a warning of danger.

Yet strong as this evidence is, it does not prove that fish are untakable at these times. The equivalent of prawns in aspic, like the liqueur brandy for the invalid, may reverse the course of events. In another book I have told the story of a pair of salmon which I found one brilliant August day in a northern stream. They were lying within eighteen inches of the surface of a tiny pool. The water was so clear that every stone on the bottom could be counted some fourteen feet below, and while the sun beat down on to the glassy surface, it seemed a long chance against a lure meeting with success. It so happened that I only had a trout rod with me, and with this and a 4x cast to which I tied a small sea-trout fly I dropped to my knees and started a stalk. The final stages of the approach were made from upstream on my stomach, leaving me lying full length on a ledge of rock within about fifteen feet of the fish. From here I was able to swim the fly down and across the stream, the nearest victim remaining in the clearest view save where the sun-glint concealed his head and shoulders. Had not every movement been made with caution (the last two yards of the approach had taken perhaps a quarter of an hour) it was inevitable I should have been detected. As it was, neither salmon showed any sign of my presence, and it is probable that the passage of the glittering little fly had every appearance of having come straight from a fishy heaven. At any rate, one of the salmon took it.

The suggestion is that if salmon are treated as the shyest of trout, they may be caught occasionally on those days which might other wise be considered impossible. In the big river, where they so seldom could be seen and stalked by the casual amateur, the high degree of stealth could in some part be substituted by using a very long line, very fine tackle, and very small flies. This I suppose is what, in effect, has been achieved by the greased line method; although I do not remember seeing it stated that fish may take the lure not so much for itself, but because the angler has remained out of sight. Given this, and a lure which is swum almost literally into the fish's mouth, and the chances of success seem to be less remote.

It is only a few weeks since I last fished the big river. Through my open bedroom window the same music of water poured in a continuous wave of sound. High up on the opposite hillside a big house was perched, the fishing lodge of the proprietor, and into it windows, too, the music was pouring. Up and down the valley the never-ending broadcast was repeated by other falls, and men and women were listening to it in their sleep. It was their river, a part of their life, and to some of them the whole of their life. As I lay and listened, I couldn't help wondering how much longer such music would be played in the highlands. In the morning, the local train would chug up the valley, bringing with it its supply of morning papers, and among their columns was certain to be fresh news of hydroelectric schemes, of fresh pollutions, of threats and counter threats to the amenities of a part of the world which, since history began, has stayed above the high water mark of progress. It seemed that the tide was creeping up. Tomorrow or the next day lorries might come rolling up the valley with labourers, followed by steam shovels, bulldozers, and all the tools of amazing and ill-omened genius to create of the river a great lake, which in turn was to give up its power to sets of turbines, from thence to be carried away on pylons across the mountains so that civilisation should have more electricity. Perhaps it was only a waking dream created by the monotony of the sound below, or perhaps the voice of the river making one last protest to a disciple. But before the sound finally engulfed me in sleep, I remembered the fate of other rivers – one strangled by a mighty dam of concrete, another choked to death by the pollution of the shipyards at its mouth, and a third killed dead by being diverted, whereby it ceased to exist at all. If this was to be the fate of the waters I have loved, I hoped in that half waking moment that I might be engulfed by the same tide to reawaken in some mountainous Valhalla, far from the bright lights of progress, where rivers flowed from their source to the sea under the eyes of a race of men who respected them.

IX

The Little River

The little river rises among mountains as remote and as rugged as those of the big river. Its birth is a gush from the loins of a royal peak and, after rain, it is as bright as a gleaming sword. A little above it, in an amphitheatre of igneous rock, the wet first gathers into a pool, to gain strength as it seeps through a bed of moss and reach the ledge from which it springs free into space. I have pried upon its beginnings through the windows of my plane, sliding down the crusted brow of its mother mountain while she has buffeted me with her gasping breath – so I have been compelled to slap the control column from side to side to remain on an even keel. Then with bank and rudder, and a throttled engine, I have dropped like a plummet into the gloomy nursery of its young life. Here it is suckled by little feeders which trace their hair lines down the carries, creating as I view them from above, fairy patterns like the skeleton of an autumn leaf.

A few miles down the gorge, a rock wall leaps skywards from the water's edge, one of the most noble battlements of these hills. It catches the morning sun, and against its side I have painted the shape of my wings as I made the turn which has carried me safely round its buttress – a difficult turn calling for accuracy in the swift flight through the defile. These first moments are colourful in their splendour, promising of great things.

Yet it is soon evident that the growing river is not to assume a mantle of kingship. Its mountain life is too short. The peaks on either hand dwindle, and it is not long before the gateway to the plain can be seen through the whirring propeller blades like a light at the end of a tunnel. Suddenly the hills have resolved their skyline into rounded curves and the lower slopes assumed an apron of pines. In another moment the gate has been passed and the river flows out into green pastures carved into orderly patterns and dotted by farmhouses. It is now that the twinkle of the sea becomes clear on the distant horizon, waiting to receive the young river, long before it has reached its prime.

From the remote pool at its source, to the yellow beaches which it parts on the coast, the distance is less than fifty miles. The area which it drains is a mere two hundred and fifty square miles. It has no fullness about it, so that it seems to remain a sprightly child until it gushes out over its bar of sand, to stain the sea. In a normal year, a bare six hundred fish fall to the rods of its fishermen and perhaps five thousand more to its nets. To set a price on the fishing, they are worth about £5,000 a year... pin money compared to the £20,000 of the big river.

As it leaves the mountains, the current slows and its curves become more generous, cradling broad meadows, and in summer enfolding fields of corn which ripple like a silken cloth in the wind. For the last twenty miles to the sea, its lowland plain is as rich as many a southern valley. Only the mountain line to the west suggests the storminess of its birth – a line which often wears its snow cap until May.

Some twelve miles up from the sea and perhaps another twelve from where it emerges from the mountains, there is a stretch I know well. Banking my aircraft steeply to follow a sweep of the river under a tree clad bluff, I reach the top end of this well loved beat. For three miles from the bend, I think that I know every bush and every stone, and perhaps every hole where the salmon lie. It is only mine by right of tenancy, but looking at its intimate features as they swing in succession past the panels of the windscreen, I feel a proprietorship over it which is stronger than casual acquaintance. Should it be my lot not to see it again before I am an old man, helped to the water's edge by a grandson, I feel that I might demand querulously to know who moved that stone or cut down that tree.

Years ago, somebody mentioned its name when I was looking for a fishing. The name had a musical ring, and within an hour I was speaking on the telephone to the proprietor. I remember how I found myself on the banks for the first time a day or two later, plunging down the river with my prospective landlord through the snow. Every now and again we would stop and my attention would be invited to the water.

'The best lie is at the junction of the streams below the island… in low water it's not much use. We come here when the gauge touches twenty inches… then it's the best place of all.'

I tried to imagine it as it would look in the summer – the tall trees laying a carpet of green up the opposite slope, the yellow shingle of the river bottom showing in place of the blue-black snow water, the thicket of the island fresh and young instead of a matted skeleton of branches, the music of the water softer and light hearted. And I could imagine myself standing here on the springy turf with the prospect of forcing a long cast to the tip of the island – and having my fly taken as it swung from the eddy into the main stream.

Pool by pool we laboured our way downstream. Nothing was too much trouble for my host, and I saw that he was a keen fisherman and probably a very good one. How good, I was to learn.

'We had a fish of forty three pounds from under that tree last year… a difficult place to fish, but always worth a trial.'

I was destined to know the tree – and most of its branches – but I never had a fish from the place.

'It's not a great river,' he continued, 'and it would be a mistake for you to come here and expect sport such as the Dee or the Tummel might give you. We hope for fifty salmon in the season and up to two hundred sea-trout.'

'Sea-trout?' I repeated.

'Oh, yes,' he said, 'there's a good run, and from June till the end of the season there's usually a stock in the river. They take well in the runs during the day… but if you care to fish at night you will probably do better.' We discussed the sea-trout prospects for some minutes and I learnt that my host often caught them while he was fishing a greased line for salmon, the small flies and fine gut giving him a double chance. But standing almost knee deep in the snow and looking down into the steel coloured water, sea-trout and warm June nights seemed a long way away. Yet the thought remained and it was exciting. Long before we reached the aqueduct which marked the lowest pool, I had decided to take a rod on the water if we could come to terms. Nor did this prove difficult, and I found myself the 'proprietor' of one quarter of the three mile stretch, a quarter which changed every half day, so that in two days I had the right of covering the whole beat.

In some of the years that followed, I was able to fly over it every day. My base was only fifteen miles away by the road, and this at the speed of a modern aircraft meant that it was only a little beyond the perimeter of the field. During the minutes which my observer required to obtain wireless permission to 'pancake', I could fly across the seven hundred foot ridge which divided the valley from my half of the coastal plain. In those few minutes I could inspect my water, noting whether there were poachers about (I once 'shot one up' until I think I scared him from that place for a long time), noting the height of the water by a stone on the edge of a pool, and discovering on the way a remarkable fund of information about the birds and beasts along the banks.

People who do not fly will scarcely realise how much of a river can be seen from the air. The most interesting revelation is the darker line of the deeper channels, an unfailing guide to where the salmon may be expected to lie. With such visual evidence, I was soon able to combine an air map which I made from three thousand feet overhead, making a picture five feet long upon which, in due course, every point at which salmon had been taken was marked.

From a few hundred feet over the water, when the river was low, the stones stood out on the bottom, and when I knew a pool to be full of fish, I searched it in the conviction that I should be able to see them. Once, in circling the Red Brae on such an errand, I wondered how I missed the crest of the ridge which guarded it. I think that my wing tip swept through a ride in the pines as my eyes were fastened on the pool below. For a brief fraction of a second I felt myself to be among the trees. .. a lightning procession of branches passing so close that for a time I was cured of the dangerous habit. Yet I never saw a fish, however close I flew, and to this day it seems inexplicable when I think of the transparency of the water.

But if I failed to find salmon, I did discover much else. The kingfisher which haunted the banks below the Wood Stream would announce itself with a blue flash of wings, the mallard on the Long Flat with her ducklings, the coot with her second or third brood in the rushes by Peter Bell, the cock pheasant who lived on the island below the Indies… all of them became familiar faces. But the most pertinent of the information was the height of the river as it was shown by the stone on the edge of the Root Pool. Years of records kept by my landlord showed that the salmon of the little river were extraordinarily sensitive to the flow of the water. A rise of a few inches after a summer drought were shown repeatedly to break a sequence of blank days. As a fresh began to go back, the salmon in the pools seemed to grow inquisitive. But it was always on a falling rather than a rising water that they would take. In my subsequent experience, there was only one occasion on which a fish took my fly while the water was still rising. It was this stone in the Root Pool which served as my guide and a steep turn above the waving tops of Pigeon Wood showed me what I needed to know. If the stone was high and dry, it was too low for fishing. If it was an island on its shingle beach, it was a time for a Number 6 or a Number 8 fly; if there was a defined current on its downstream side, it was a moment for a bigger fly still, and when the first white plume of water broke about its flanks, I knew that my best chance was with a bait. Only when a black swirl marked its place and the stone itself was invisible, did I know that I must stay at home.

Then straightening out my aircraft, I would lift it over the brow of the guardian ridge and slip down on to the long black runway, my mind already back on the water and a rod instead of a control column in my hand. If I made some bad landings as the result of my preoccupation, I was still often climbing the wire fence which guarded the pool within seventy minutes of leaving it by air.

My first fish on the little river were three kelts which I hauled out of the Long Flat while the snow still lay heavy on the ground. Their size – about fifteen pounds each – at least gave me an idea of what I might expect later on. It was still February, and I had anticipated nothing. Clean fish were reputed to refuse to run the ice cold weirs, and like all fishermen on the middle reaches we were waiting for the temperature to rise before unleashing our hopes. In that first year, I had to wait until April before I hooked a salmon, and then only once in the years that followed was it otherwise. Then I took a magnificent fish on the third day of the season.

It was the seventeenth of February, and the snow on the mountains was dissolving fast. I had taken out my rod for the first time that year, hoping for the chance of playing a kelt, and certain only of the pleasure which the feel of a rod gives all fishermen at

the beginning of each new season. The water was running high –
sixteen inches up from its summer level, and as cold as charity. I
hadn't been casting for ten minutes when I hooked a fish under the
bluff of the Red Brae. I played it solemnly for a few minutes, with
more courtesy than a kelt deserved. But I wanted to feel the urge
of a salmon again, the vibration of its body, the shake of its head.
Then tiring of the make-believe, I forced it ruthlessly downstream
to a quiet flat where I could tail it, and send it on its way again with
my blessing and thanks. I was so certain that it must be a kelt that
towards the end I man-handled it with the intention of getting rid
of it, only to bring my heart into my mouth as I saw it for the first
time on its side, drifting towards the little bay I had chosen for
lifting it out. The deep curve of its belly, the radiant silver of its
flanks, and the proud head startled me. My eyes might have still
doubted the evidence, but my feet didn't. I plunged into the river
and placed my body between the fish and its freedom, lunging at
its tail with my open hand. With a feeling of disaster, I missed it,
and for a second the fish thrashed the water about my knees. But a
second lunge was better aimed, and with its tail end in my grip, I
flung myself and the fish on to the bank.

There I stood looking at it, convincing myself that I wasn't
dreaming. There was no doubt about it. Here was a clean salmon of
some fifteen pounds, a net mark on her back which couldn't have
been more than two days old. I dispatched her, and sat down on the
bank, thinking with horror of my recent efforts to shake her free.
Later, while the fish still lay beside me, I looked at her again. Never
before, to my knowledge, had a clean fish been caught so high up
the river so early in the season. But this was not the only cause of
the strange doubts which began to assail me again. The fish had a

wrong look about her. Years of association with the little river had implanted notions in my head about what one of its spring salmon should look like. As a farmer can tell the difference between one breed of sheep and another, so I recognised a difference between the salmon which ran the water in the spring and those which came up in the autumn. It was a subtle matter of colouring, of shape, of the carriage of the head... and this was an autumn salmon if ever I saw one. I had seen her peers too often not to recognise the qualities.

So I felt her teeth, and finding them well developed, was convinced that all was not well. I slit her belly immediately, and discovered her eggs within a month of ripeness. The solution was plain... I had a salmon who had forgotten the date. She should have been here the previous autumn, and through some slip in her fishy intelligence had failed to arrive until mid-February. Now, hurrying to the head of the river, she would have spawned out of season, and if a male fish was running with her, there might have been some fry to puzzle a burn fisherman at the back end of the year. To make doubly sure, I scraped off some scales for examination, and in due course they helped to confirm the theory. She was a five-year-old lady who had missed the last bus!

In that first year, the river ran eighteen inches above its summer level for eleven consecutive weeks. Never within living memory had there been such a winter, and it was mid June before the last of the snow melting's had reached the sea. One day in April, after I had been a 'proprietor' for seven weeks, I drew first blood. It was not a long time to wait on the little river, and in later days I was to know bigger gaps between one fish and another. But the dogged, almost inhuman patience which small waters demand was, at that time, wearing my patience thin.

As a first fish, it was a memorable one. I saw it at the junction of the streams where they closed about the island above the dam. It was a big fish, not an ounce under twenty pounds, and the colour of it was in startling contrast to the tarnished kelts. It jumped two feet clear of the purple black flood, and as the first salmon which I knew for a certainty was not a kelt, my spirits rose. The golden sprat which dangled on the end of a wire trace looked good to me, and it seemed as though it might also look good to the kingly monster out there in the river.

It was an easy cast from my stance on the grassy bank, but I hopelessly bungled it. The tangled brushwood of the island was only twenty-five yards away, and a few yards from its point the sprat should have landed, to swim gently across the lie. But while the bait was still describing its arc through the air, propelled by a finger of lead which might have felled an ox (a heavy lead was needed in this torrent) I knew that I had miscalculated. It was the kind of mistake which more often than not loses an angler the chance of his fish... it landed right on top of him. The white splash of the lead as it touched the water looked big enough to scare the salmon out of the pool and catching the line in a panic, I began to recover it quickly in the ridiculous hope that if I was only quick enough the fish wouldn't notice the assault. The line didn't come in very far. In the first yard it was solidly checked as though the barbs had sunk into the trunk of a tree. Just for a fraction of a second I didn't understand. Then out of the black flood leapt a bar of silver. It was a wild, shuddering leap, which brought it back into the water flat bellied and with a splash which I could hear even above the steady roar of the flood. Simultaneously, the rod point was smacked hard down on to the water and the handle of the reel whipped from my fingers, to strike my knuckles on its first furious revolution.

This was a fair introduction to the fighting qualities of the inhabitants of the river – although hardly a usual one. I had foul-hooked the great fish in the back, a piece of luck I owed to an incompetent cast. The fish made off downstream into the wide pool above the dam which, today, looked more like a lake. Never, I think, have I known a fish move so fast. Every ten yards or so, it jumped, and once I saw the gleam of the sprat pinned like a gold ornament to its back. For the first fifty yards I was able to follow – glad enough to keep pace. But then a line of bushes effectively called a halt. In a normal water, it would have been possible to take to the river, but at this level the risk was unthinkable. I was left with the choice of holding tight in the hope that nothing would break, or of taking the strain off the fish by peeling off the line faster than it was moving. I chose the latter, for the trick had worked with a foul-hooked salmon before while the construction of the reel I was using enabled me to swing the drum in an instant so that the line was free. For a second or two, the coils whipped upwards and disappeared through the rings with a sizzling swish. Then they stopped, and the line hung slack, drooping down into the water with perhaps a hundred and twenty yards off the drum. Somewhere along the dark line which marked the lip of the dam the fish had turned. But now there was no sign of it – only the smooth flowing water, heavy and ominous.

There was nothing to do but to wind it slowly back. A score of yards were recovered without a check, and then another score. As I continued reeling in, a momentary pull suggested a sunken rock, but the line slipped over it, and more and more came in. But now a dead weight was offering a steady and increasing resistance, as though the line had bellied downstream while the fish had moved up again against the current. If this had happened, I was in luck, for the pull of the water was now behind the salmon, and it was more than likely that it would continue away from the strain – upstream. Then without warning, the water parted opposite to where I was standing, and I had a full view of the salmon once again, some thirty yards away.

Within a matter of seconds the strain was renewed, and with a rip the line cut through the water. This time it travelled upstream, slower, and I followed it easily. There was an anxious moment as the fish tried to pass to the far side of the island, but I pulled it across the river by brute force. The hold of the hooks should have broken free at that moment, and because they held I felt certain of the fish. I forced it clear of the point by a bare rod's length, and had it in the torrent of water twenty yards away. Now the current was doing the fighting for me and I saw the fish begin to drop slowly back. As it came I eased it across the channel to my own side. The gaff was already tucked under my arm, and I hoped to whip it into the fish as it passed. The chance was a good one, and the easiest I was likely to have. Yet with only ten yards separating us, the fish seemed to renew its strength. I matched it with greater pressure, and for a minute we balanced each other's pull like two teams in a tug of war. It was a battle that couldn't last. No salmon could withstand that current and the strain which I was putting on it. It came in towards me from above. With a yard or two to go before I reached him with the gaff, it was necessary that I should still further increase the strain, applying it vertically to bring him to the surface. The flight of hooks with the sprat came into view, and I was just reaching downwards and outwards, forcing the last foot required, when the hold gave. I could scarcely believe it. I saw the salmon hanging momentarily in the current beneath my feet, and I had just realised that if I was quick enough I could still get the gaff into him when he sedately drifted away.

First blood – but not very much of it. A piece of flesh the size of a sixpence and half a dozen scales were impaled on the barb of one of the hooks.

June came round at last, and with it the possibility of a sea-trout. So far the river had taught me little except the difficulty of getting salmon out of it. Towards the end of April a spring fish of eight pounds had seized a minnow and had been successfully landed. Then I had had two more on the fly in May, the best weighing a mere twelve pounds. It seemed a small return for the energy I had expended, for I had not yet learnt that the yield of a river such as this is rarely to be measured by the number of salmon which it produces. Yet now that June was here I looked forward to sport more often, and as the month came in with a flood, I had high hopes that the first sea-trout of the year would have arrived. On the third of June the entry in my diary verged on the emotional:

'Oh reluctant, horrid little river!' I wrote. 'I wasted a gallon of petrol on you today, convinced that you would repay it. Do you remember that when I flew over you this morning, you showed me your stone half uncovered and its shingle beach already partially clear? You had it hidden yesterday under your brown flood, but on your own reckoning you were, today, in perfect order. Deceptive wretch!

'I was clever, too. Looking down from three hundred feet, I estimated that the gauge would be reading twenty-four inches. It was actually reading twenty two inches when I arrived four hours afterwards... which proves that I've learnt to sum you up well enough from my aeroplane. Tyndall's was looking perfect, but you never showed me a fish in its long, tumbling channel. In the Boat Pool you were actively hostile, presenting my minnow to a rotten log you had freshly clasped to your bosom. At the Red Brae I thought, at least, that you would change your attitude. Of all the pools, I doubted whether you would have the effrontery to hide your treasure here. But you did — until just as I was packing up my rods. First came the slither of a sea-trout — the first of the season — a couple of yards behind me, then a salmon another ten yards back in water I had just covered, and lastly another salmon twenty yards below... one after the other, as though you had relented at last.

'And you know what you did? You persuaded me to fish the pool down another three times... twice with a fly and once with a minnow... and you sent me home so exhausted that I was unable to eat my supper. Oh, horrid little river! Why don't you

be sensible and surrender – for you surely know that I'll have
the better of you in the end.'

At the time I really thought I should get the better of it. I
thought I should be able to catch fish because I should discover
the size and shape of the lures and the manner of fishing them
which these peculiar salmon fancied. All I ever discovered were
two incontrovertible facts, both of them useful, but neither of them
short cuts to success. One was simply the lie of every salmon in the
three mile stretch at every fishable height of the river – a useful
enough piece of information if I had been willing to go for them
with a gaff, a 'snigger', or a stick of gelignite; and not without its
purpose when fishing under difficult conditions with a fly. The
second was a doleful certainty that there were days, many days,
when fish could be presented with every artistic creation of the
trade without the slightest chance of one of them being tempted.
Of course the big river had these moments too. But there were so
many more salmon to every pool in the big river that the exception
might be present to prove the rule. In the little river you could say
with a degree of certainty, whenever the water was low, the number
of salmon in each of the twenty pools. It would be rare to discover
more than ten together, and generally there were only two or three.
In some of the pools, for some of the year, there were lies which
were without a tenant at all. I considered these to be satisfactory
reasons why I caught less than a dozen salmon in the first year.
    It was the sea-trout which kept me on the water. When there
are such sporting fish in a salmon stream, it is they as much as the
bigger game which will tempt the angler to return again and again.
The relationship between the two always seems to be the same as

it is between wild geese and duck. When you have failed to stalk the one, you can often 'flight' the other, enjoying the compensation of the lesser game with unspoiled relish. Of course there were sea trout to be taken in the big river, but the ghillies up there spoke little of anything which weighed less than ten pounds, so that a visitor naturally spoke little about his prospects of the smaller fish.

But in the little river where there was no hurling to distract the true fisherman, no boats, and very few ghillies, the capture of a sea trout was almost as pleasurable an event as the capture of a salmon. Sometimes a fish would be taken by chance while a salmon lie was being covered, and on the light rods and fine casts we used, the sport was excellent. But I preferred to make a special assault on the sea-trout, either by night, or when the river was a few inches above its summer level and otherwise neglected stretches came into their own.

One evening during that first year I was walking up the high grass bank which leads to the Long Flat, and as I approached its lower end where the water was wide and quiet, and no more than thirty inches deep, I saw in the translucent amber of the stream, a score of dark shapes which came to life as I moved. It was obvious that I was disturbing a school of sea-trout. They could only recently have taken up their residence for they hadn't been there two days before.

I sat down on the lip of a rabbit hole to wait while the fish recovered from my too obvious arrival, and while I waited my landlord came down the bank from up river. He thoughtfully made a wide detour of the place where the trout were lying, and came to sit down beside me.

'That's a school of sea-trout,' he said, seeing for himself the reason for my interest in this usually uninteresting place.

'I know,' I said, 'but I don't just see what I can do about it... unless a dry fly would tempt them?'

'It might,' he said, 'but the water is very clear.'

I knew only too well what he meant. How many times had I not stalked sea-trout under similar conditions, and even placed a floating fly with delicacy over the nose of a fish without rousing its interest. A chalk stream monster of the highest intellectual development was an uneducated lout compared to the intelligence of many sea-trout under similar conditions.

'The river is up,' continued my landlord, 'I think you'll get them later.'

This was quite true. The river was clearing after a small fresh and the last of its colour still stained the water.

'They'll drop back as the light fails,' he went on. 'I think you'll get them in the stream under the bushes on the far side.'

This was interesting advice, for the stream was an unnoticeable trifle which drained the deep pool above it. It ran for a couple of hundred yards under the north bank of one of the widest parts of the river where the whole of the south shore was a light-hearted shallow which went tinkling over a bed of pebbles. In low summer water the channel under the bushes seemed to have no more weight

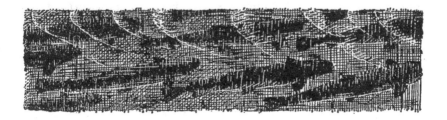

than the rest of the wide stream, although today it certainly had a darker and more purposeful flow.

Very soon my host went back upriver to fish a higher beat and left me to contemplate the prospects ahead. The sea-trout were back in their lie and hung motionless like dead sticks close to the bottom. It was useless even to fry them. So far I had had a good day, and I felt that I could afford to wait. I had accidentally run over a hen on the way from my base and I had negotiated the purchase of a dozen eggs. Both prizes were secure in my bag. If I failed to add a fish to the score, I should still have no reason to complain.

Half an hour later the bag was further enhanced, this time by a hen pheasant. It looked as though it would turn out to be a very unusual evening. It was certainly an unusual pheasant. It darted for shelter into a rabbit scrape under the bank of the Wood Stream, whither I had gone to cast a fly pending the arrival of darkness. I retrieved it from its shelter and guessed that it had something stuck in its throat. I had heard of pheasants which had choked themselves by a glut of seed and subsequently died of starvation. This one seemed to be an example, and it now reposed at the bottom of the game bag, very much alive, and apparently unperturbed. I intended to 'doctor' it when I reached home.

There were still no fish to keep it company by the time I returned to the sea-trout. In the failing light I peered into the shallows at the tail of the pool and could not find them. Perhaps, as my landlord had predicted, they had already dropped back into the glide below. I fished the tail down with a pair of small salmon flies without result, and moved on into the glide which followed. Twenty yards down a trout took me with a wholehearted grab, and out in the dim light where the sky glinted on the stream there was a bold splash. It had been lying close in to the far bank in water which was probably not usually more than two feet deep. I played and landed it a sea-trout of two pounds.

During the next hour, I hooked eight other fish and landed three of them. The current was swift, and the wide river demanded my longest line – so that I know the flies were skating fast across the surface as they swung towards my own bank. But each of the fish were in no way put out, and followed the lures to take them with enthusiasm time after time. I took home in my bag that night four sea-trout, one hen, one pheasant and a dozen eggs. It was an occasion on which the little river did me proud.

On several subsequent occasions there were sea-trout to be seen at the lower end of the Long Flat, but unless the river was high enough to persuade them to fall back into the glide as darkness fell, they were very difficult to catch. I caught them in a really high water in the deeps of the pool itself, and sometimes in the broad shallow at its tail when it was quite dark. But whenever the river had the magic extra height, I had magnificent and easy sport in the glide. At no other time did this water yield me a fish, and at no time did I see a salmon in it.

When autumn came, I had a partner on the little river who, until that year, had never fished. We went together to offer combat to the bigger and better late running salmon which invaded the river on the October floods. His appetite for a salmon was insatiable and as each week went by without it being satisfied, it began to be a race between the closing season and his hard plied rod. Many a time he deserved a fish, for he was learning the lies, the art of casting, and all the things which an experienced angler hardly knows that he knows. Then one day he came home to tell me that he had hooked and played the biggest salmon he had ever seen, and that I must immediately come out and get it.

The unusual part of his story was that the fish was in a place from which he said it couldn't possibly escape. Between two pools there was a rough shallow, and halfway up the shallow a pot, little bigger than a full sized bath, which had been eaten into the bank. The salmon had been trapped in the pot, possibly seeking temporary shelter while the river had been high, and finding itself marooned by delaying its departure too long. Certainly no one had ever reported a salmon in it before, and I have never seen one in it since.

The story opened when my partner had been accosted by two boys with the report that an enormous fish was jumping in the hole. He had walked down the river, and seen for himself that it was true. With commendable speed he had thrown in a fly which had been immediately seized. Thereafter there had been a battle in which

my partner had suffered a decisive defeat. The fish, being unable to leave an area which measured roughly ten feet by six, stayed where he was and defied all efforts to tire him. Finally the hold of the fly had broken and my colleague had returned to listen patiently to suggestions that next time he tried a few well placed rocks thrown into the river coupled with quick use of the gaff.

Shortly afterwards he hooked another fish, and once again had to return home defeated, disappointed, and yet more determined than ever. This time he had cast out a bait from between two trees which stand at the lower end of the Kingfisher's pool. Ordinarily, it is not a place where one expects a salmon. But the river was in flood, and under such conditions an occasional fish lies in the stream of a normally calm and shallow flat.

He found himself attached to one of the big salmon which come up in the late autumn, and with no stronger a link than a thread line and a multiple reel of light construction. All went well for the first few minutes. The fish cruised sedately over the broad waters giving the angler a chance to set the check on the unfamiliar reel and settle down to what he thought might be half a day's sport.

Then the fish decided to swim into the next pool downstream. A twenty-pound line and a stiff rod might have stopped him. A complete removal of all the strain by peeling off line faster than the salmon was moving might have had the same result. But to hang on and listen to the steady buzz of the pawl while the line dwindled, was to adopt the attitude of a rabbit confronted by a snake.

'It was a horrible feeling,' said my partner.

The thought crossed his mind that if he threw himself into the water and clambered out on the other side of the tree, the situation might be saved. He would have tried this, so keen was he to get his salmon, had not the fish changed its mind with a few yards to go.

Now it came upstream towards him, and better still swam slowly against the current, right to his feet under the bank, as though it were spent and victory was to the angler. The gaff, with its telescopic sections, was already an urgent problem – first to unsling it and then to extend it – when the salmon took a closer look at his captor. He jumped, flinging his whole length clear of the river, and so close that my friend alleges that it touched the point of his rod.

It was a misfortune for which there was no repair. The line snapped, and the biggest salmon which he had yet approached closely, went free.

But if the little river was hard on beginners, it could also be extraordinarily kind. For weeks it would stubbornly refuse to yield a fish, even to my expert landlord, and then one day it would, as it were, throw a couple at the head of some beginner. It happened twice to guests of mine. On the first occasion I had taken the novitiate to the top of the high bank overlooking the dark pool of Tyndalls and adjured him to fish it down carefully with a small fly. He had with him a beautiful new spinning outfit and a box of minnows, but I secured a promise from him that he would not attempt to use it until he had tried the fly. The river was low, the water gin clear, and the day bright. I left him there, while I went downstream to try the Red Brae with a sea-trout fly and a greased line.

It was perhaps two hours before I returned without having seen a fish. The novitiate was sitting on the bank with a grin on his face while he puffed at his foul looking pipe. Hidden in the grass beside him were two salmon which he had taken on the ugliest looking artificial golden sprat which ever darkened a flood. His fly rod was still in its case.

The second occasion was four years later when a Canadian member of my squadron gave utterance to the extraordinary statement – for a Canadian – that he had never seen a salmon in its native element. I invited him to accompany me on my next assault, warning him that I hadn't had a salmon for nearly two months and that I doubted very much whether he would have more than a distant view of one today. When we reached the river we found it clearing after a big flood, and still some twelve inches above its normal summer level (the month was June). But in the placid deeps of the Boat Pool (it goes without saying that there was no boat on it) we found half a dozen fish jumping. Some of them were showing far down the water where it broadened and shallowed before it charged into the bank guarding the Red Brae. They were obviously running, and my doubts whether we should hook one were increased.

The Canadian put up his five ounce trout rod, refusing to use my own more suitable implement. Then he insisted that I fish the pool down ahead of him. I did this with small flies – it was surprising how the salmon preferred a sea-trout size during the summer, even when the river was high – and about thirty yards down I got into a spring fish. In landing it, I struck it so hard with my gaff that I opened the hook, and capped the piece of clumsiness by breaking the hook from the shaft by using it as a priest to complete the kill.

So far, my friend had not put his fly into the water, but now I insisted. While I effected a temporary repair to the gaff with a reel of sticking plaster, I saw him throw out his line into the calm deep water at the head of the pool. The line floated. It was evidently a greased trout line which he had used in his native Canadian rivers. I thought to myself that he was probably a pretty good fisherman, for it went out long and straight, and instinctively I saw that he was using the greased-line salmon technique, taking a step downstream to prevent the line from dragging. There were two fish showing in front of him, both of them a little red, and both of them covered by myself a quarter of an hour before. His chances were poor.

At the second cast there was a thrilling splash, and in a moment the little trout rod was bent double. The ensuing ten minutes were breathless. Had they been broadcast, they would have sounded like the closing stages of a world title fight with both contestants only just on their feet. In spite of my advice and heady encouragement, the Canadian worked his fish beautifully in towards the bank, and after two abortive yells to him to hold it up while I used the gaff – on each occasion followed by a furious run of the fish – I got the point deep into its side. The salmon was on the bank.

Never before, and probably never again, am I likely to see a novice catch a salmon at his second cast. Nor is it likely that I shall meet a trout fisherman who had a better appreciation of the power of a small rod and knew how to use it. He said that he had caught heavy bass with it in his native lakes – but whatever the explanation of his ring craft, he killed his fish as quickly as I killed mine, and there was not half a pound in weight between the pair.

A few days afterwards the rain was coming down again, and a number of fishermen were gathered round the stove in my squadron office. One of them was a visiting pilot who had been flying in Iceland, and he told how he had watched the previous year two local anglers at work on one of the famous rivers. At the end of the day a cart had come along to collect the catch.

'I counted eighty salmon put into the cart,' he said, 'and then I lost interest.'

He would prefer my little river.

X

My Secret Loch

There is a little loch in the north which has probably not been seen by a hundred living Englishmen. It is likely that there are others in this same remote area of the highlands which could claim a similar distinction. But this is my particular loch. None of my friends have found it, although a few lay claim to other remote lochs as though to offset my own treasure. They are welcome, and I've no doubt that their waters are as good as mine. In the counties of Caithness, Sutherland, and Ross and Cromarty, there are hundreds of tarns which might interest a man with a taste for his own company. Every one of them have trout in them some of them a few trout of enormous size, others many trout of a very small size. They remain unvisited for weeks, and perhaps months at a time, by virtue of the difficulty of reaching them. We in England have conservative ideas about travel and a point on the map which is more than half an hour's walk from the nearest motor road is safe from all but the most persistent sportsmen.

The climb to its stony shores is a stiff one and the hollow in the hills where it lies is not easy to find. Nearly a thousand feet below is a track which the handful of men and women who live along the valley dignify with the title of road. From its nearest point to the loch the distance is about three miles, and a further three miles on the valley is joined by a second glen where for the first time it is broken by a pattern of small fields, a few cottages, and most important of all – an inn. If you happen to be a resolute motorcyclist and a fair walker, the journey from the inn to the loch can be made in a hundred minutes. It is another hundred minutes to the nearest town of any importance. By common standards it is an inaccessible place. Yet by taking off from an aerodrome on the east coast and flying a north westerly course as the aircraft is climbed over the mountains, the loch is revealed in its hollow in less time than it takes to walk the length of Piccadilly. By these standards, it is only a stone's throw from Edinburgh, although a landing is out of the question.

It was April when I last visited it, a wild month common to the difficult birth of spring in the north. The clouds were stirring uneasily about the waist of the hills, spreading a dark roof over the water – a roof which rose and fell to the order of a capricious wind. The scene looked deathly, with the heather a rusty brown and the bog holes as black as night and the boulders glistening blue-grey in the damp. It was no day for fishing.

As I toiled over the final shoulder of the final hill I was met by a hurricane of wings. Every mallard, widgeon, teal, oyster catcher and stormbound gull rose with a lamentation. That speck, slow moving, unarmed, but best hated and most feared creature in all nature was at the gate – a man. The man was glad enough, of course, for the sooner the birds were off the loch the sooner would the fish settle down after the commotion.

It had been a long time since I was here and the feeling it gave me was a strange one. If you have walked up the main street of your home town ten, twenty, thirty years afterwards, you may have had the same feeling. Every step was a jolt to the memory, and I found myself smiling at familiar things I never hoped to remember.

I had come alone, and as can happen at such times, I found myself talking to a second and separate ego who walked beside me. In the emptiness of the hills it seemed natural. So as I walked round the boggy shore I said: 'Do you remember this clump of rushes? This was the place where a few mallard always stayed behind. Ah… there they are,' and with a rattle of brittle stems a flight of six birds was climbing to join the armada overhead. They gave me the feeling of meeting old friends again, and when a final pair lifted heavily out of the tangle, it seemed a certainty that the laws of time were set at nought. As the birds rose I knew what they would do. They would fly low round the north shore and come back overhead within easy shot. Had they not done it before, rising from behind that broken stem? Almost immediately the wings were beating towards me low over the headland, and with a shrill whistle of pinions – which is among the most lovely sounds in the world – they swept by within thirty yards. I could see the gleam of the light on their emerald heads and what looked like the flicker of gold in their eyes... surely the descendants of the pair I had startled years before?

In a few moments the mallard were climbing in widening circles. The topmost skein was half in and half out of the mist, perhaps two hundred feet above the water. Now they were little more than shadows although the sound of their wings still came down as a rushing noise like the draw of the tide on a quiet beach. I thought for a while that they would return, so I sat on the tip of the Long Point and waited. But once disturbed, mallard seldom return, and then only in the wildest weather. They wheeled and disappeared eastwards between the shoulders of two hills.

For the moment I had almost forgotten that I had come here to fish, but now that the loch was quiet again it was time to think about it. I reminded myself that it was April and that the wind was cold; and then looking across the quick ripple, bare of any rise, I began to realise how stiff was my task. A loch which lies so high above the sea is no place for a fisherman early in the year, and even in the Lowlands on such a day there would be a poor chance. So I crouched with my back against a boulder, watching, until my thighs were stiff. There was never a movement, and never a sound save for the call of an occasional cock grouse and the never ending harmony of the water on the stones. Rather than freeze, I put up the rod and uncoiled the best cast I knew for such days... a Peter Ross, a Greenwell, and a Hardy's Gold Butcher... and with this I went into the south bay. It was desperate work, savage casting in the cross wind which swept through the hills, and soon my fingers were numb through drawing in the wet line. Then I tried the Temple Bay where a granite pillar stands like the Statue of Liberty off the north shore, and still I saw no fish. So I tried the east side where the ground is level and the water shelves over a shingle beach. Here the brown froth was piling up against the stones and blowing it in light flecks on to the heather where it waved and bobbed like cotton seed. It was difficult casting, and only by cutting the rod point hard down on to the water was it possible to get out a line at all.

Few sporting occupations can pall so quickly as flogging the dead surface of a loch, and I only continued because it kept me warm. I could have exchanged the flies for a minnow – but I had resolved not to spin until the afternoon. A thread line on an open loch is a poor enough pastime when you are catching trout; when you are not catching them, the procedure savours of a game of patience which can never come out. Nevertheless I was about to surrender to its questionable charms when a trout jumped. It was the first I had seen that day and it threw itself a foot out of the water twenty yards from the shore. It must have been a trout of half a pound, which is a good fish for this loch. The cascade of silver which followed it back into the waves raised hopes and deferred the decision to spin. In another ten minutes there was a stir in the dancing water to my left, and when it was repeated a moment later it was confirmed as a rising fish. The flies were sent out to cover it but they returned untouched. Yet something was happening...

something besides these odd movements. There was a feeling of change in the air, and soon I knew it for a rise of a few degrees in the temperature. The clouds still swirled overhead, dropping now and again almost to the level of the water itself; and the wind still blew. Yet it had backed a point or two, and the rasp of its breath was softer.

I moved again to the head of the loch where the water shelved more steeply from the shore and the wind was in my favour. Here also I saw a trout move, to be followed by another and another. It was not a sensational rise, but in half an hour I had seen a dozen fish.

There was one which was breaking the surface continuously off a bed of reeds where a tiny burn fed into the loch. It was rising in the deep channel, and repeatedly I covered it with my flies. With equal persistence it declined to notice me, and went on rising.

During the next two hours I dropped several different patterns of fly over what ought to have been a basket of trout. During that time I also sacrificed my dry shod feet to recover three possible clues from the surface – a dark winged olive, a March Brown, and a curious opaque creature which looked like a transparent stick about half an inch long and which might well have been the uni-cell organism from which sprang the human race. On one of these the trout must be feeding – although in the ripple it was impossible to see which. Yet it was evident that even had the information been given, I should not have benefited. It was one of those occasions when the fisherman was defeated before he made a cast. The only definite piece of information I gleaned off that unproductive and infuriating period was that the fish were feeding from a specific depth of water. They were not in the shallows, nor in the deeps, but beyond the ledges where the water was between six and eight feet.

It was cold comfort.

The afternoon was wearing late and the probability that the rise would be over at any moment made my fishing increasingly urgent. It seemed ridiculous to return home with an empty bag after so many chances. So I tried the minnow. I mounted one on a wobbler, and so as to retain some sort of an illusion of sportsmanship I used the fly rod. It was a highly inaccurate weapon through the uncontrollable whip of its top joint, but it hardly mattered. The thread line sang through the rings and the bait could be cast downwind for nearly thirty yards without the addition of a lead weight.

At the first cast there was a pluck. For a moment I scarcely believed it. I had fished for so long that I had arrived at the state of mind which discounts the possibility of actually catching anything. I thought that the bait must have snicked a sunken rock and broken free again. But at the second cast there was another unmistakable check, and this time a fish had a hold, and proved it by running a dozen feet off the reel. I played the victim as though it had been a salmon hooked on the same light tackle. After an interminable interval it was brought over the lip of the net and lifted tenderly on to the shore. Its weight was perhaps six ounces.

An hour later the fourteenth trout was lifted unceremoniously out of the water and swung on to the bank. There was no more finesse about my tactics. Long since it had become a case of hauling them out as quickly as possible, pouncing on them, and returning the minnow to the water with the least delay. If the mist had not come down like the premature fall of the curtain on a good play, the number of trout I should have had to carry across the hills might have been remarkable. The only way to avoid catching them was to bring in the bait fast. If it was spun slowly, every trout within range went for it as though his life depended upon it – as indeed it did. The biggest fish was a monster of nearly a pound – bigger than anything I had previously seen in the little loch. The average was between a quarter and half a pound, save for the few babies which had been returned. They were in nice condition, which was a just tribute to an open season.

A strange thing remained to be explained. Half the trout in the bag had been feeding on the surface. I had seen them rise and then fished for them, as though I had been using a dry fly. Every time the bait was brought across the path of such a fish it was seized. I do not remember another occasion when fish feeding on the surface took such an interest in a minnow. It had been a remarkable day – after a start which was as unpromising as the weather itself.

It was time to go home. The pillar rock was scarcely to be seen through the mist thirty yards away. With the lowering of the blind the wind had dropped – or perhaps it had been the other way round. There was now a deathly silence which made one conscious of one's own breath; the sound of a displaced pebble was magnified, the call of grouse somewhere on the hillside was like a voice at one's elbow in the night. Even the small sounds of the water had gone. I wasn't anxious, for there were at least four hours of daylight remaining and I felt confident that I could find my way back into the main valley. I found one of my own footsteps in the soft peat where I had approached the loch in the morning, and set off with this as my mark.

Two hours later I was wishing that I had sacrificed the last half dozen trout and started earlier. I was standing knee deep in wet heather, wondering which way to turn. A light, persistent rain was falling, as though the air itself was composed of more than half water. It had soaked everything from my outer clothing to the inside of my shirt. Yet it was not this which annoyed me as much as my lost sense of direction. There had been an old and dim track which broke away to the left nearly an hour before, and I was just becoming aware that I should have followed it. The ground was rising again instead of falling, and now even the thin sheep trails were failing. I was in an ocean of five-year-old heather punctured here and there by lichen-crusted boulders gleaming in the drops of rain. Anything more than fifty yards away was shrouded in the mist.

There was nothing to do except to retrace my steps as best I could, but anyone whose Eustachian tubes have once failed will realise how impossible it is to win back a sense of direction. When I came to a sheep track I followed it, trying to keep a downhill trend. But as I went on, panic began to creep upon me. You can't be alone all day and then lose yourself without becoming momentarily unstable. It was ridiculous, of course, for there was nothing alarming about even the prospect of spending a night on the hills. I was tough enough, and it wasn't really cold. Yet I could not help the feeling of being encased in a sort of tomb. The mist and the cloying heather and the boulders all seemed to stand stubbornly in the way as much as to say: 'You can't get past.'

Soon afterwards I made up my mind to walk downhill, wherever it might lead me. It seemed satisfactory until the ground levelled off and I found myself on a plateau of heather pitted with bog holes. It was then that a breath of wind suggested that here at last was a signpost which might be useful. If the wind hadn't changed, then I knew now which was north and south. Visualising the map, the conclusion was that I had been walking at nearly ninety degrees to my proper course. I wanted to go south, but the wind said that I had been walking west. As the wind was the only guide available, I decided to trust it, and changed course accordingly, now walking with it on my right cheek.

It was getting dark, the mist had a deathly greyness about it – when I thought I saw something move in the gloom ahead. I was apparently on a steep hillside, for the ground fell sharply on my left, and whatever I saw was on the other side of a huge boulder which grew out of the hill some forty yards below. I stood and listened, and then suddenly there came the soft thudding of many feet, growing closer every second, as though a ghostly charge of lancers was almost upon me. The hand which gripped the strap of my bag was wet with more than the rain when the things came out of the mist in a swift, leaping procession. The nearest of them passed within twenty yards, close enough to see the smoky breath from its

nostrils. They were red deer. Then up by the boulder there leapt a magnificent stag – the shadow in the mist which I had first seen.

I sat down in the heather shivering. It was irrational, of course, but the long walk, and the swift approach of darkness, and then these leaping shapes from another world did something to me over which I had no control. It must have been some minutes before I pulled myself together, and then when I looked up I saw another shape, upright, and looming enormous in the mist which had suddenly closed tighter around the hill. This was almost too much for me. If what I had first taken for ghosts had proved to be only deer, there was at least no mistaking the character of this figure. I don't know what fishermen are supposed to do when they are benighted on a moor and meet with a spirit. But I think that I was about to scream when a broad Scottish voice inquired whether I was lost.

I got up, and my knees wobbled as I moved towards him. I put out a hand and he steadied me, and in a moment I was as sane as I ever am. I was looking into a pair of the palest blue eyes... almost all I remember of him... and firing questions one after another.

'We'll get away home,' he said without answering. 'It's not easy walking on the hill in the dark.'

So we went together, while I gradually understood that I was on the wrong side of the watershed – in the next valley which joined my own some four miles below. Somehow I had turned round, climbed to the level of my loch again, and had headed north to cross the hills which I was now descending. My companion was a keeper who had been visiting an outlying part of his estate, and it was he who had put up the deer and sent them driving towards me through the mist. It all seemed so logical when he explained it.

'You can never trust the wind when you leave the high ground,' he was saying. 'It takes queer shifts when it gets into the valleys. On this hill', he went on, 'you'd think you'd get the wind in your face if you climbed it in a westerly... but it comes out of the south from a big corrie on the opposite slope...'

It was all but dark when we reached a stream at the foot of the hill, and we followed this down until a track grew out of the rough ground. As we dropped lower the mist thinned and the darkness seemed less intense. Far away we saw a light, and after what seemed an interminable age we came to it and passed it, and saw other lights beyond. Finally we stopped at one of them, and my companion turned in through a door and I found myself suddenly in a brilliantly lighted room with a fire and a table with a white cloth and a bust ling woman who helped me out of my wet clothes.

To be out of reach of the clutches of the hills and to sit hunched over a fire, hypnotised by the flickering flames, and to sip strong tea to which something stronger had been added, and to hear the murmur of voices in the background, was indeed good. Out there beyond the deep black patch of the window was something which I felt had nearly got me. How totally untrue this was did not matter. I had once felt the same about a fog-bound sea when, belly to the water, I had flown my aircraft safely back to base and wallowed in the warm comfort of the dry land and just such friendly voices. Neither episode had any real danger attached to it – only discomfort, and the anxiety which leaves the mind half-drugged when it is lifted.

The voices droned on, and I heard an exclamation of surprise from the woman. She had discovered my trout, and turning round I saw them slithering from the bag on to a large white dish. They were all wet from the rain and glistening as though they had been newly caught. I felt proud, and as the blood pulsed warmer through my veins, I began to boast about my luck. The man drew up a chair and we lit our pipes, while in the background the clink of plates presaged a meal which, every moment, I was feeling more ready to enjoy. Three of my fish were to be split and fried, and when the pinkness of their flesh was noticed and remarked upon, I accepted it as another personal compliment. While they cooked, we talked of fish and the hills and the way life went at the head of the glens.

Long afterwards the woman brought a mattress from another room, some blankets and an old rug, and I made up a bed close to the fire. Neither would hear of me attempting to reach the inn that night. It was four miles down the road to the junction of the glens, and another three up the opposite valley. In the morning, if the mist had lifted, I could take the short cut across the hills. My clothes would be dry by then.

It was easy enough to be persuaded, and when my hosts retired to their own room I slipped out of the borrowed garments, turned down the lamp, and curled up by the light of the fire to sleep. The last sound I heard was the gentle hiss of the rain on the ground. The last thing I saw was the glow of the fire on my eyelids.

XI

Roddy

Roddy came into my life softly through the trees. He was
suddenly there, sitting on a stone like an idol that hadn't
moved for a thousand years. A dozen yards out in some heavy
water were two salmon, small summer fish lying within a yard of
each other high up in the feed to a pool. The water was not more
than three feet deep and by getting the light at the right angle it was
possible to see their outlines.

Neither I nor the figure on the stone took any notice of each
other, and it was no concern of mine if a spectator cared to turn
himself into a graven image on the bank.

The problem of the fish was an interesting one, and incidentally
one unlikely to be solved. The river was low and clear, and if it
hadn't been for a heavy shower in the night I shouldn't have gone

out to fish. Even now I realised I had misjudged its effects, for the water was within an inch of the previous day's level.

The salmon had probably been in the run since the last good rain ten days before, and almost certainly they had only come from one of the pools immediately below. It required a big rise to bring summer fish from the estuary, and even then a high level had to be maintained if they were to have the chance of running the weirs.

Consequently, few salmon could be taken in a dry summer, and they were always difficult. Like other rivers of its kind, the good times were during the melting snows of spring when a sprat or a big fly might tempt them, or in the autumn floods when the larger fish came up.

Experience showed that the best tactics against a pair of fish lying in fast, shallow water on a summer day was a small low water fly, dressed short, and fished close to the surface with a greased line. The day being dull, a darkish dressing seemed indicated, and I had put on a variant of a Blue Charm which had yielded results under similar conditions. It had a standard wing, but to the usual black body a flash of yellow floss had been added.

I wasn't altogether a novice at this game. On those occasions when success had come my way, the tactics originated by Mr Wood of Cairnton had proved their worth and persuaded me that I was a qualified disciple. If the chance was slender, it was certainly a chance. The fly was fished faithfully from above on fine gut, dropping slowly down and across the current as I 'mended' the line and added to the floating slack. I tried the lie a second time from almost opposite, for sometimes a fish will rise to a different presentation. I had even a faint hope that the pair might be grilse – for I had seen grilse lying close together like this before – and if there's one thing about a grilse, it is its readiness to take a lure when its elder brethren won't look at it. But I had no luck.

After a brief rest I tried the lie a third time with a much larger fly, and then finally with a little silver-blue sea-trout pattern. Long before it had swum its course, I realised that it was hopeless, and I was thinking that my only chance would have been first time over with a prawn.

All this time the figure on the stone had not moved and I was slowly walking away when a voice halted me.

'It's a pity to leave them,' he said – and it was then that I observed him in more detail. He had a bush of raven-black hair above a face which was burnt to the colour of walnut by the sun. It was a face like an Indian's, and the way his body melted into the stone as though he was a part of it gave one a curious sensation. But his brown eyes had a yellow sparkle, and there was a hint of humour round the corners of his mouth.

'It is a pity,' I said, 'but what would you do?'

'I'd hardly know – the water's that low, and those fish have been in the river too long.'

'Do you think a prawn would be any good?'

'Aye – a prawn might be good – but you fished them well enough just now I doubt there's nothing doing.'

I doubted there was not, and once again I began to move away when the voice followed me.

'Would you care to lend me your rod, sir?'

Well – why not? It would be pleasant to rest on the bank while my odd looking companion showed what he could do. He took the rod, examined the fly, bit it off, and solemnly handed it to me. In its place he produced a hairy monster from his waistcoat pocket and tied it on with little more than a flick of his wrist. I had never seen a man tie on a fly quicker and I think he used a single jam. Then walking upstream he said:

'I always prefer to get further away from a fish than you do, sir.'

He could prefer what he liked, as far as I was concerned, though I was surprised to see just how far upstream he actually went. If he was going to cover the fish from there, he would have to make a remarkably long cast. This he did, after a few preliminary swishes. He threw a beautiful line, driving it through the air with all the power in the rod. (It was only a single-handed sea-trout rod). Then I saw one of the fish rise. It was the faintest movement on the surface of the water, barely discernible. But it had definitely followed the lure. He made one more cast, and then reeled in, and walking back down the bank, handed over the rod with grave courtesy.

'Thank you, sir.'

'You turned him over,' I said.

'Aye –'

'Well – isn't he worth trying again? There seems to be a chance.'

'Not that fish, sir.'

While he was removing his fly from the cast, he said quietly, as though to himself: 'I see you fancy the greased line – many gentlemen prefer it these days.' And then after a pause: 'I never did well with it myself.' His tone implied that no one else was likely to do well with it on this river.

'And what do you do well with?' I asked.

He looked at me and said with slow deliberation: 'If I wanted one of those fish, sir, I should take it in a way you wouldn't like. It would take me about ten seconds.'

I interpreted an invitation in his voice, and before I stopped to think, I'd offered him a pound.

'I never take money for fish,' he said, shocked. And then before I could change my mind he added: 'Give me your rod again, sir – there's no need to lose the sport.'

He dived into a capacious pocket of his jacket and produced a bundle of cord with something that gleamed in its middle. On unrolling it he revealed what is known as a 'snatch' – three cod hooks soldered back to back to form a triangle, their common shank wrapped with sheet lead, and an 'eye' bound in for fastening the cord.

'It's not a thing I care about over much,' he said. 'It shows poor sport unless it's worked on a rod – and a rod is a conspicuous thing at such a time.'

I nodded, while he began to tie one end of the cord on to my line after removing the cast.

'I thought you said it would take only ten seconds,' I said.

'It'll take less than ten seconds when I'm ready, sir.' His dark head was bent over the knot, but now he looked up and began to coil the cord round his hand. 'You'd better get your watch out.'

He moved down to the river's edge – glided down, for his feet didn't seem to make any sound on the stones. For a second he seemed poised as though about to jump – staring at the water ahead of him. Then his right hand shot out, and the triangle described an arc through the air. It fell with a little splash, upstream of where I thought the fish to be, and perhaps a yard or two beyond. It seemed almost certain that the fish must be disturbed, and my faith in the result departed. Now holding the cord as though it were a high tension cable which might electrocute him, he began to pull it towards him, holding it almost by the tips of his fingers. He seemed to have recovered about six feet when his hand swept back and his shoulders twisted, while in the middle of the river there was a sudden commotion.

'He's hooked about the tail, so look out for yourself,' he cried.

Hooked he was. As my companion threw the last of the cord into the water the strain came on, and the fight opened with a mighty leap, and a race down the river.

'Ten seconds,' shouted Roddy. 'Man, it was not more'n five!'

He was mightily excited, and frankly I was excited myself – excited by the prospect of the fight, and at my connivance in the deed.

Ten minutes later it was all over and a female fish of eight pounds lay on the shingle at the lower end of the pool. It will seem a short time for the killing of a foul-hooked fish on a sea-trout rod, but when the rod is held low and at a narrow angle to the strain – with plenty of line drowned in the water to absorb a sudden shock – the killing power of a rod is doubled.

We stood looking down at our capture like a pair of felons. It was a bonnie fish, perhaps three weeks out of the sea, and with no sign of maggots or discoloration.

That it should lie there so serenely when such a little time before it had seemed so unattainable gave me a feeling of unreality, as if a conjuring trick or a miracle had been performed. Surely fish could not always be taken from a river with so little fuss? Surely the moment was unique in the annals of fishing?

'Maybe we had better go back and get the other one,' said Roddy.

That was the beginning of our acquaintance. I came to know him later as a remarkable poacher. He was, too, the first human being I had met who had a real, although unconscious understanding of the wild. It made him a naturally brilliant stalker, so that he could get up to a fish or a bird or a stag almost with the same easy nonchalance as the ordinary man could approach an old lady who was asleep. His capabilities impressed themselves on me as he brought me time after time up to one quarry or another without it suspecting our interest. There was magic about it, as though his personality radiated waves which drugged the senses of any wild thing which he was approaching. He was, of course, never impatient, or angry if some plan failed to materialise. His ability to accept a defeat was on a level with his ability to wait. He could move like a ghost, and was the only man l have ever met who could cross a patch of snow on a still day without apparently making a sound. Long reeds melted before him, the branches of trees parted, twigs bore his weight, the pebbles on a river bank solidified under his feet. Where I would be impatient to rush the final approach, he would be slower than before, and when he was in position he would not hurry to shoot, to cast his line, or to do any of the less orthodox things he loved to do. Instead he would lie and watch his game, happy in the look of it, and secure in the knowledge that it would stay where it was until he condescended to kill it.

His story is a strange one, and parts of it have little to do with what I have been writing. Other parts are no credit to either of us. The trouble with Roddy was that he didn't know when to stop. He would go on hunting until he had game for all his friends – while there was a fish still remaining in the pool or a bird in the wood. He never to my knowledge profited by what he did, and very rarely would he keep anything for himself. His delight was in the chase by which he proved himself to be a cousin to the birds and beasts and fishes which he hunted, and, like other cousins in the wild, a dangerous relation.

He came to ghillie for me on many occasions, and in this capacity also acted as my guide. Within an area of many square miles around the place where I met him, there was not a stream which he did not know, or a wood which he had not been inside, or a moor across which he could not find his way in the dark. Scandalous as were of his practices, he had friends everywhere, some of them masters for whom he had trodden the straight path of temporary gamekeeper. Maybe their friendship and patronage had been inspired by the knowledge that his goodwill was a protection for themselves many for he would not poach the estate of a friend... or at least not to excess! Maybe they liked him for his own sake, as it was difficult not to do. Whatever the reason, Roddy made me many new friends, high and low, and if the other story which I tell of him resounds neither to his credit or mine, it is to confess how I learnt another trick rather than to set a crime at my friend's door.

One hot summer's day, Roddy and I were fishing a broad stream of tepid water, and without prospect of success. Towards evening Roddy, who was acting as ghillie, was approaching that stage when a departure from the orthodox style of fishing was inevitable. The signs were an increasing restlessness and a wandering attention. Half a dozen times during the day we had found a fish, or rather Roddy had found it, with his amazing eyes, and we had tried for it with all the cunning we possessed. It had been to no purpose. The river was low, the salmon stale, and the weather oppressive. By lunchtime I knew in my heart that we would carry home an empty bag. Then Roddy decided otherwise.

'How long is it now since you had a fish?' was Roddy's opening gambit.

'About six weeks,' I said, 'and it looks like being another six before we'll get one.'

'I think we ought to get one now,' said Roddy.

I handed him my rod, and followed him when he set off briskly upstream.

'This way, sir!'

We went up the bank for a few hundred yards, past the two pools we had first fished, to a broad shallow into which he plunged without regard to his trousers. We crossed to the other side and went on upstream over a grass field, until he stopped and gripped me by the arm.

'Now, sir, we'll get ready here.'

My ghillie always became respectful when dark work was afoot, and I realised now that the straight and narrow path was already far behind.

'You need a fish, you say, sir well – that's quite all right, if you just leave it to me.'

I was weak, of course, and most blameworthy to refrain from making any enquiry. I could see the anxiety fading from Roddy's eyes – although I hadn't an idea what he intended to do.

Fifty yards away on our left was a slow deep pool which we had only tried in a perfunctory way earlier in the day. It was too slow, and too clear, unrippled and utterly without any redeeming features. Salmon lay in it frequently, and there had been two fish moving that same morning, one just below the bend at the top, and the other halfway down beneath a small bush. The line had fallen lightly enough across the twenty yards of mirror-like surface from the opposite bank, and with infinite slowness the fly had swum over the place where the salmon had moved.

'I doubt that we'll be lucky,' Roddy had said. 'I've never seen a fish taken here with the water so low.'

I hadn't realised until then that he knew the pool – that his knowledge of this part of the river was, in fact, encyclopaedic.

Now I realised that we were to do a thing which I should subsequently regret, and when I saw Roddy unsling the gaff from his shoulder and drop to his knees, the worst was disclosed.

I protested and was rewarded by a savage 'hist' from my accomplice, he was now gliding towards the top of the bank and I was left standing twenty yards away, holding the rod.

He had slowed his snake-like approach as he came to, within a few feet of the small bush – the same bush I had noticed that morning. Hang the fellow – I couldn't stand here alone and watch murder done. If there was to be a crime committed, I would at least be a witness. So I subsided also to my knees and followed him.

I had never before seen a salmon removed from its lie on the point of a gaff. It is an operation lightly considered by free thinkers as an easy one, to be performed nonchalantly by rogues whose clumsiness has baulked them of their quarry by more legitimate methods. Judgement of distance, timing, to say nothing of consummate stealth, play their part. Let no one tell me that poaching a fish is a pastime for beginners or imply that the average angler could do it if he didn't happen to be such a sportsman.

Roddy parted the branches of the bush as though it had been stirred by a zephyr and froze into immobility as his head hung two feet above the water. I was lying by his heels for several minutes before he moved.

'He's downstream another yard,' said Roddy. 'You can come up beside me when I'm ready, but take time.'

'What's he like?'

'A bonny fish.'

He would say no more, and he left my side without apparently disturbing a blade of grass. This time he slipped under an arm of the bush till his black head came to the edge of the bank from which it began to grow outwards no faster than a shadow. It was a long time before I was up beside him. When I finally looked down into the water I could see nothing. There were the sides of a short row of old railway sleepers receding away into perhaps five feet of water, and then a bit of root protruding from the bank above, but beyond that there was only an opaque brown nothingness, a mixture of reflected glint from the sky and the mud from the bottom.

'Two feet out, three feet down,' said Roddy. I still couldn't see anything.

'Under your nose,' he said patiently.

I stared long and intently into the water, and suddenly the salmon was held clearly in my sight so that I couldn't understand how I hadn't seen it before. It is like this so often with the amateur observer. He doesn't know what he is looking for. A salmon to him is a gleaming bar of silver and he forgets that when looking down upon it, it is no more than a grey shadow.

Having seen it, I was all anxiety for immediate action lest it moved away. But Roddy knew better. He had to satisfy himself that he could get the gaff into the water and underneath him without disturbing a twig or a blade of grass. It seemed ages before the dull steel hook was sinking an inch at a time through the water. Before that, his body had been slid further out over the river so that he was more directly above his quarry. Down and down went the hook. The refraction of light made it seem that it was going the wrong way, and when I whispered, 'More to your left,' all I received in answer was another savage 'hisst.' And then it suddenly happened – so quickly that it was impossible to observe. At one moment he was lying full length, and the next he had exploded like a coiled spring, twisting upwards and sideways so that he was half on his back. And I saw then that the water which had deceived me as to its position had also deceived me about its size. The fish was no ten pounder, as it had appeared, but nearer to twenty pounds. Maybe Roddy himself had been deceived, for its weight suddenly overbalanced him and his feet came up like flying flails, and long before I could grab his heels he was himself in the river. And the most vivid impression left behind was of the tendons of his wrist standing out like rods as they kept their grip on the gaff.

I had him by the hair within a second, and in another second by the collar of his coat. For a moment I thought he had hurt himself, until I realised he was still having an underwater grapple with the

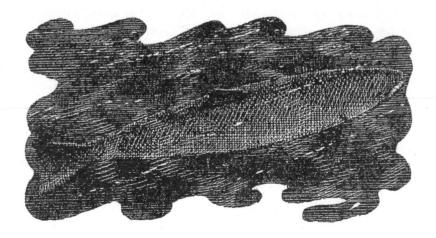

fish. I got my foot on to the butt of one of the sleepers and a hand under one arm, and then with a strength which surprised me – and probably surprised Roddy – lifted him clear of the water and on to the bank in one sweep. But by far the most surprising thing of all was the salmon clutched to his stomach, held tight by the shank of the hook across the outside of its body and with the point still in its side.

We walked away from the river that evening with a feeling of self esteem which must have brought a glow to the heart of the devil. Damp as Roddy remained, his spirits soared to a level where the confession of past crimes tripped from his tongue like a demon fledgling. I began to see how black was his soul, and how disarming his philosophy. More than ever before, he showed that the sport of poaching appealed to him above all else. Was there not a rare spice to the risk and a just reward for skill? It was most regrettably true, although I did my best to deny it and to warn him of the inevitable consequences. His eyes only looked into mine with a mocking glint. I was a fine one to talk, they said. And as they flashed the message, his voice promised gravely: 'I'll never do it again.'

XII

The Burn

There should be a burn in every fisherman's life – and preferably at the beginning of it. When he is too stiff to crawl and too old for hard manual labour, it will be too late, although it may still teach him more about fishing than he ever dreamed was possible. A burn is a poor man's paradise and an education without a rival.

I have enjoyed comparative poverty and good fishing at the same time. The great salmon rivers were then only legends, and the famous trout waters were unattainable except for an occasional invitation. The story of the burn belongs to a different age from most of this book, but it is more a part of it than any other experience, for it taught me about fishing.

It is a long time since its small music last fell on my ears, but it lies softly on its bed of memories. The hump backed bridge and its utterly impossible pool guarded by a forest of undergrowth and roofed by the timbers of big trees was the first and the last I saw of it.

It spanned about two thousand days in time, and a score of feet of exciting water. For a mile below I came to know every inch of it.

I discovered it on a June day just before sunset when the light was piercing the trees like sword thrusts through the spirit of dusk. I had just traversed thirty three miles of sun washed moorland in rather less than thirty minutes. I had ruptured with disregard for life and limb the sanctity of June's golden peace, riding a two wheeled juggernaut at peak revolutions in an ecstasy of speed. It had brought me satiated down a swift hill on the hollow sounding echo of a perfectly tuned engine, and I had come to rest against the parapet of this bridge.

Now anyone who has passed through a storm of sound, whether on the ground or in the air, will enjoy the cup of peace in proportion. This particular cup seemed exceptionally good. As I leaned over the bridge the creak of a cart going home added that age-old poetry book conception of peace which in spite of everything that the writers have done to it, still tastes good. What was now attracting me was a trout rising in the centre of the pool just clear of some enormous soup plate water lilies. I was speculating on its size when the owner of a pair of clumping hob-nailed boots said 'Good evening' as he passed.

'Does anyone ever fish here?' I asked, and the hob nailed boots paused. I was confronted by a round, very red face, capped by a shock of flaxen hair which stood up like a stook of ripe corn. The eyes of course were blue – Anglo Saxon blue, common in those parts. Their owner was perhaps thirty-five, and I guessed that he had been hay-making.

'The kiddies sometimes fish,' he said. 'They're not worth catching.'

I thought about that, for lots of people hold the view that small fish are not worth catching, and it is a view I never shared. We talked for a moment, and then I accompanied him round the corner under the trees to a grey stone inn which lay on the fringe of a hamlet hidden by more trees. We were in one of those valleys where a gathering of stone houses forms the nucleus of a rolling sheep country. In terms of civilisation it was composed of a general store, a fifteenth century church with a squat grey tower, and this inn where ale was put away in remarkable quantities by nearly every male inhabitant. The inn had a long, low roofed kitchen with a massive table of undressed oak down one side and a grey parrot with a red tail in the window – but I only discovered this afterwards when directed towards a plate of home cured ham garnished with eggs. Before that I had become acquainted with the two people who were to play an important part in the rise of the burn. There was the dark eyed, quick moving Jenny, whose grandfather had left her the inn five years before, and who had come up from the south to manage it. They say it takes ten years to get to know these northern folk, but however that may be, Jenny had succeeded in much less. Then there was Charlie Farrell of the big boots and corn-coloured hair – the first person I had spoken to in the village. I was to see

Charlie throw a bull which had attacked him in the middle of a field before I left these parts. He worked the farm through which the burn flowed, and he was to become my friend as well as my landlord. Charlie could lift a two hundred pound sack of grain on to his back with one hand, and sometimes when I passed through the yard on the way back from the stream, he would evidence some incredible feat of strength like a child showing off.

But I go too fast, for that first evening I drank a quart of brown ale with Charlie and after a diffident request to Jenny for ham and eggs, or anything else she'd got, I wandered off down the burn by myself. It was during the twenty minutes it took Jenny to prepare the meal that the idea was conceived. It didn't come all at once, of course: it grew like any other child.

I went down to the burn leisurely, out of respect for the brown ale, and in the stillness of the slanting sunshine, the charm of the banks laid hold of me. A little below the hump backed bridge there was an overgrown gully through which the stream rushed with a merry sound. And below it the water split on either side of an island. If there were no trout here, I thought, there ought to be. Then for another fifty yards the burn flowed below the back gardens of a row of three labourer's cottages. Thereafter it burst out into the first of Charlie's fields, now full of cattle, its course lined with thorn and alder bushes. Forty paces down there was a sharp bend with a spit of dark sand and a bent willow on the inner side. Then came a cattle ford, and after that a cut with a ten foot clay bank on one side and a forest of rushes on the other, with the water a yard wide in between.

I am conscious of how little justice I do the charm of these banks. The meadow with its stream between the enfolding hills, and the slow smoke of the village is not a canvas for a quick sketch. Nor did I see it for the moment as anything but the background to a pleasant trickle of water which might provide an amusing afternoon's fishing.

'Are you sure there are no decent fish in the burn?' I asked Charlie when I returned for my supper.

'Why don't you come back and try for yourself?' he replied. He had an enormous jar of ale at his lips and his blue eyes sparkled with goodwill as he looked at me over the top of it. It was then that I definitely decided to return. I had seen a score of tiny shapes dart under the protection of the banks as I had made my way down the stream, fish about four inches long which moved with the speed of light. But in the willow pool, and where the stream divided at the island, I felt sure that there must be bigger trout. So I accepted the invitation, and the following night I was again eating up the moor land road which led from the big town where I lived. This time I carried a four ounce burn rod of seven feet, and a 5x cast with a box of blue duns, red spiders and olive quills. I didn't see Charlie or Jenny, but I met a bent old twig of a man smoking a stinking black pipe over the top of the gate into the big field. He was Charlie's general hand, Jock, and I afterwards knew him for two remarkable qualities. He could spit further than any human being I've ever seen, and he was the only teetotaller in the village. As against this, he gave the appearance of being an evil-tempered, drunken old reprobate.

He drove the cart which brought our stone from the quarry Sunday after Sunday, and had I never paid him a cent I believe that he would not have given the omission a second thought. The generosity of his temper knew no bounds. If you were a friend of

Jock's, you were a friend indeed. But at that time I knew him not at all. I passed him and his black pipe with a nod, and crossing the field, got to my hands and knees below a little bath tub of a pool.

I fished upstream till in the blue dusk the lights in the village were blinking like stars. Four fish rose to a small Dun in the bath tub, and thereafter I must have risen fifty more in the narrow channels and the little runs of the next three hundred yards. I learnt this evening how difficult were these tiny trout to catch. Unless you struck quicker than summer lightning you missed. If you did happen to be quick enough, the fish as likely as not would be flicked out of the river to crash land ten yards in the field behind. It was many weeks before I learnt how to twitch the wrist with just sufficient force to drive home the tiny barb and still leave the trout in the river.

I took eleven little fish. They weighed less than two pounds between them, and the biggest was just three ounces. By the time I got back to the inn the doors were shut and a single light in an upper room suggested that it was already bedtime. So I mounted my juggernaut and drove back supperless over the moor, slowly, while I made plans for the burn which I had now determined to make my own.

The first thing to do was to find a partner – and I knew I would not have to look far. There was a deep-voiced hook-nosed fellow in my town who was so thin that I was never sure whether he was a freak, or just starving. For a guinea or two he fought losing causes on the local circuit as a barrister. His weaknesses were a passion for justice and trout fishing – and he was as violent in his pursuit of one as he was gentle in the other. Over all he had two great possessions a battered motorcar and a tolerance for my company.

So on the way home I made up my mind to put a proposition to lawyer Joe.

Because this is the sort of proposition which can still be made by one impecunious angler to another, it is perhaps worth giving its substance in some detail.

I've found a stream, I said in effect one of the tributaries of the River X which as you know is quite good. This stream is about ten feet wide in its expansive mood, and three feet wide where it narrows. The banks are mostly mud or clay, as high as twenty feet in one place under a hill, and mostly between three feet to eight. There is every conceivable sort of snag from thorn bushes to enormous beds of rushes. But it's full of small trout. They're very small, but I think they could be made to grow larger. There's a pool which looks about four feet deep under a hump backed bridge where I think there may be a half pounder – though Charlie says there isn't. And there's a pub and one or two nice looking people. What do you say to five pounds a year each – after you've seen it, of course?

Joe came out the next night, and I rode beside him in his car. On the way I tried to remember the other things about the burn which I hadn't mentioned. The Willow Pool and the bath tub were the highlights. I reckoned them to be six feet deep, although virtually unfishable until the bushes had been cut back, and a fallen tree removed. Then there was the calm stretch, almost like a canal, which ran between the high reeds – there must be trout in that, and if it's current could be speeded up a little it would not be so difficult to fish.

But I waited Joe's verdict until he had seen for himself – a viewing that lasted a long time and only found expression after

Jenny had cleared away more ham and eggs than we had seen for a long time.

'It's got possibilities,' he said. 'First of all, those small trout have to be taken out. There's too many of them; there's not the food to go round. Those little fellows may be four or five years old – I'll get some scale samples next time and see for myself. And the whole bed needs cleaning – no oxygen. That means weed cutting and the construction of at least half a dozen dams and as many piers. Bare essentials, my dear chap. Where do you think we can get some stone?'

Joe was under way, so I didn't answer him.

'We'll need water-snails and shrimps – old Gorman's the man – he'll tell us what new weed to plant and he'll sell us the snails later on. Might even get a few yearlings from him – not more than a hundred... just to give the place a drop of new blood. It'll be a good little stream in about three years.'

Joe ran out of words and drained his tankard. There was the light of enthusiasm in his sombre eyes. We'd talked of this sort of stream before, but we'd never even looked like finding it.

Jenny came in to set an oil lamp on the table. Then she covered the parrot.

'Is Mr. Farrell in the bar?' I said to Jenny.

He was, and Jenny went out with a message for him to join us. Charlie Farrell came in and cast a shadow on the ceiling that looked as big as a battleship. He shook Joe's hand, and wrapped the other round one of the quart tankards which Jenny kept specially for him. And then we got down to business. Charlie didn't want any money, but we jointly insisted on ten pounds for the absolute fishing rights, pointing out that by the time Joe and I had broken our backs over the stream it would be worth at least fifty pounds a year and probably a hundred. Our tenancy was forever – if we wanted it – and he, Charlie, was to be the unpaid watcher.

Charlie thought we were mad, but he had a generous tolerance as witnessed by his employment of Jock with his unique views on alcohol. The bargain was struck and Charlie heaved his great bulk off the opposite bench, blotting out the light for a moment as he disappeared through the door to the bar.

'He moves remarkably easily for so big a man,' said Joe. 'Did you notice the way he dodged below the lintel – like a great cat. If he took those boots off, he wouldn't make a sound.'

And I did notice it. Afterwards I used to watch Charlie, particularly when he came with us to the quarry. That was in the following spring when we were making the first of the dams. Some of the stones were too big for us to lift on to the flat cart, and it was then that Charlie was consulted – which meant that it was Charlie who was to do the lifting. A smile would break across his round red face like a cloud passing from the face of the sun, and he would follow us down the road without a word. When we came to the quarry and showed him the stone, he would look at it with blue eyes suddenly very solemn, and then as though he had made up his mind how to grasp it, he would bend down and with apparent ease pick it up. Only occasionally would he have to use our rope, and make a cradle. But I came to appreciate the natural grace with which all his movements were endowed.

We never signed an agreement. There was never a piece of paper exchanged between us. Joe didn't like agreements for all his lawyer training, and as he pointed out, you could never bring a man like Charlie Farrell to law. It would be like trying to get a lion into a rabbit hutch.

We didn't make our stream all at once. We didn't make it in a year – or two or three. But we evolved a sort of book of rules by which its emancipation should progress, and as it progressed should yield us continually improving sport. One of the unwritten laws was that Saturday. afternoons and Sunday mornings should. be devoted to work, leaving Saturday evenings, and the rest of the day after noon on Sundays for fishing.

That first year saw a few small results, among which was the verdict of Joe's piscatorial friend who pronounced the water

suitable for the introduction of snails and fresh water shrimps. It was a big thing this, for an increase in the food value of the water was bound to govern the success of everything else we did.

Before we stopped fishing in mid September, the population over the whole mile of water was substantially reduced. Over four hundred small trout had been removed, and credit for most of them went to Joe who developed an uncanny knack of hooking four out of every five which rose to his dry flies. I never managed to hook as many as half my own rises. The biggest trout was caught early in September, and it too fell to Joe in the Bridge Pool. I believed that it was the same trout I had seen rising that first evening in June. It was a prodigious fish of exactly five ounces. No other trout came anywhere near it for size – although we had seen another, more sensational still, which had not been caught. This was a fish we christened 'Charlie', after our landlord, and if it weighed an ounce, it weighed three quarters of a pound Charlie lived with his nose up against the drain which led from the Vicarage and fell into the stream through the undergrowth on the north bank below the bridge. There was a little channel hollowed out in the bed of the stream on the far side with the pipe feeding into it, and when we heard that the village had just got a new vicar, we decided to leave Charlie alone to see if he would grow any more. He did. He was a fish of fully one and a quarter pounds when we saw him for the last time three years afterwards. But apart from Charlie I don't think there was another big fish in the whole stretch. There were one or two which we saw lower down which might have been a quarter of a pound, and one in particular which I hooked and lost in the Devil's Throat below the footbridge (a couple of planks for the benefit of the sheep) which might have been a fraction more. But taken all round, that first year didn't yield a trout which we would have cared to show any of our friends.

On the works side, five hundred yards of stream were roughly cleaned from the point where it broke out of the trees into Charlie's big field. That is to say, about a ton of rushes had been dug out and flung clear of the banks – while the dross of years from sizeable tree stumps to matted and rotting branches freed the current in a dozen places. It was a wet and dirty job and called for thigh waders and garden forks. The black mud which gathers round the roots of rushes had a hot sweet scent of decay, and we didn't like it. But the job taught us much about the bed of the stream which we shouldn't have otherwise learnt. It was mud, with occasional outcrops of rock, and where there was a good current a light layer of clean gravel covered the bottom.

In August we planned out the sites of three of the dams and two of the piers. We foresaw one of our pools as a noble stretch of water almost the size of a golf green – something of such proportions that it was going to be a full length cast for our burn rods. And when indeed it was completed and had successfully withstood the floods of three winters – when after all this it showed itself unwilling to hold a fish of more than a quarter of a pound, while the average for the whole stretch had risen to nearly six ounces, we were still proud of it, and let our visitors bathe in it. It was on the downstream side of the pool that the work paid its dividends. By this time the overflow had decided to leave the pool through a gap which it had made for itself on the south side, and the force of the water had undercut the bank below and hollowed out a small but deep pot five yards lower down. Out of this pot a guest took a trout of fifteen ounces in the spring of the fourth year.

Anyone who talks lightly of damming a stream even as small as ours revises his language very quickly. Where the job is concerned with clay banks the problem can be viewed with distrust, and by no one more so than by the landlord, who may wake up one morning to find that his estate has expanded or contracted – maybe by a whole field – through the inadvertent redirection of the stream. An ill-chosen dam may in a winter flood collapse – better so this than the bank which holds it to its course. Even Charlie would have demurred at the rearrangement of his farm. This was a misfortune we both escaped, but only through the constant renewal of the piles with which the banks were reinforced where the wall of a dam abutted the clay.

It was a lucky chance that brought the dam building within the range of practical politics. We had decided early in our tenancy that the dams were essential, but there was not a stone of a decent size to be found anywhere near the burn. We seriously discussed buying a roofless cottage which had been burnt out years ago and which stood just outside of the village. It was built of stone – as were all the houses round about – and we reckoned there was at least six good dams in its fabric. But the owner priced it at £20, which in those days was a great deal of money. Instead, we accepted as a gift from Charlie one great stone – a sort of foundation stone de luxe – on which to build our hopes. Even Charlie needed our help to raise it. It had been lying in a corner of one of his fields a four sided block, six feet long, which would have brought a sparkle to the eye of the Stonehenge contractor. In the days when men made things to last, it had been a gatepost, and two holes had been bored through it. Joe was so enthusiastic that he was carried away into telling a downright lie – that he was able to manage a horse. Charlie produced the horse, and between the three of us we dragged the stone to the river bank and got Charlie himself to push it over into the water. It lies there to this day, the least scientific of any of our works, but one of the most effective. The push that Charlie had given was well judged, for it fell half way across the stream, forcing the water into the opposite bank, where the current formed a splendid lie for fish during the storms of the following winter. In fact, it was in that lie just a year later that I caught my first trout of half a pound. It was on this occasion that Charlie commended us to John Wilson who owned a quarry about a mile further up the valley, and so enthusiastic did he become about our building plans (he wasn't the slightest interested in the fish) that he said we could have his flat cart and Nellie – and Jock if he felt like it – on Sunday afternoons.

We waylaid Mr Wilson that night, and his stone cost us two gallons of beer and two sore heads.

It was cheap at the price.

One evening in spring, Joe and I sat on opposite sides of the oak table in Jenny's kitchen. The fire glowed ember red in the grate and the oil lamp threw soft shadows behind the beams. The parrot was covered up and the voices in the bar were a distant murmur. There was good reason for us to be feeling at peace – for we had just completed the first dam and capped it by eating a four pound chicken which Jenny had specially killed for us. Joe, loaded to the plimsoll line with good things, looked up over the rim of his tankard and asked humorously:

'What precisely have we been doing?'

The question sounded out of place until I thought about it, for every joint and muscle in our bodies shrieked that we had been manhandling large lumps of importunate stone. What Joe meant was why had we been doing it, and it was for the answer to this question that I searched my mind. At that time I didn't know. Our labours were built on faith rather than scientific knowledge.

'Was there anything wrong with the stream when we found it?' he added.

'It looked wrong,' I said. 'It needed dams.'

Joe gave me one of his dark brown stares which he reserved for witnesses who were lying, so I repeated the assertion another way round. 'The stream was too sluggish – it needed aerating.'

It was then that Joe addressed me as 'me learned friend' and told me a thing or two I suspected before. Streams are not aerated by building dams, nor are they speeded up. The things that dams and piers do to a river are to make pools and create places for fish to shelter from strong currents. It seemed that we had been wasting our time. But had we? We drank seven more tankards of beer and arrived at a decision. Then we went home easy in our minds. On the way we were stopped by a policeman on a bicycle for having only one sidelight burning, and as Joe couldn't trust himself to remain upright on his feet should he get out to inspect, he gave birth to the classical if irrelevant observation: 'Thank God I'm a teetotaller.' And so we drove on.

We had agreed in our tankards that the dams and the piers were going to be all right. We didn't really know why, but we were sure of it. We had a sluggish bit of water, but we had cleared so much weed out of it that it was faster than it had been. And for some of the newly created fast stretches we had already reserved the out-size rocks from the quarry. They would surely provide lies for the monster trout of the future and a gathering ground for gravel? Gravel is important – or at least Joe thought it was. Our session produced other immediate decisions, too, among which was one to purchase five pounds worth of water shrimps and a sufficient number of snails to start a snail farm. Old Gorman had recommended these, so we knew we were on sound ground. We actually became the proprietors of these desirable trout foods within a week, and the farm was given its official opening in a little creek fed by a ditch just above the cattle ford. No one who has not before had the management of snails can understand the joy they bring to the owner. Unlike most other amateur attempts at breeding livestock, they multiply and do everything expected of them without the least trouble or labour. Half a barrowload of broken crockery and flower pots canvassed from new friends in the village and deposited in the creek was the sole foundation of our and their prosperity. Subsequently transferred on bits of broken saucers and soup plates to the bed of the stream, they provided increased rations for innumerable trout – so much so that by the end of August we were catching the odd quarter-pound fish almost every Sunday afternoon.

I was never sure about the success of the shrimps. Shrimps are unreliable things outside chalk streams, and are prone to curl up their toes and pass away. I would back a water-flea for a good life against a shrimp any day. Our particular shrimps were distributed impartially throughout the top five hundred yards of the water (upon which we were concentrating) but subsequently they were to be found only in a half a dozen stretches among the water cress.

But the snails – ah, the snails were, within two more years, on every stone in the gravel behind our monster rocks, and in the weeds. The menu for the month of May in nineteen hundred and whatever it was... the third year of our tenancy... had a West End extravagance about it. In addition to the snails and the shrimps, there were the larvae of stone flies, March Browns and May Duns, while in due season there were caddis-flies, water-lice, olives, skaters and in the slow deep bends, masses of putrid-looking soufflés variously known as plankton. And on top of all this, Joe imported about half a hundredweight of frog spawn from a neglected pond in the Vicarage garden (an act blessed by the

Vicar and consecrated by Joe with an inaccurate rendering of the Cassius speech over the body of Caesar). These things are rightly allowed to be good for trout, and when a visitor took a fish of nine ounces out of the Bath Tub in July of the second full year, the point seemed proved.

It was really remarkable what improvements the stream ·was showing. Without putting another trout into the water, the average size increased in three years from less than three ounces to more than six ounces. Our first alcoholic conference had set a mark to our ambitions – an average weight of half a pound. But by this time we were looking to an occasional pounder and an average maybe of nearly three quarters. What luxury – what luck, if we could realise it.

The second and biggest and, as it turned out, the last dam was duly completed. There were a dozen tons of stone in it, faithfully carried by Nellie piece by piece from the quarry. The wall had leaked like a sieve at first, but clay from the banks, backed by small stones from the bed of the stream and sods ripped from the field, had closed its pores, and now there was a noble stretch of water to fish.

Nineteen piers and groins had additionally seen their inauguration. We grew to like the piers more and more, first because they involved only about one tenth of the sweat and tears of the dams, and later because they paid the better dividends. In cutting off three-quarters of the flow, they directed a strong current into the opposite bank which in turn went to work for us in a most satisfactory way. Banks were undercut (and unfortunately collapsed from time to time), and deep holes were formed as new channels were scoured. In a stream whose average breadth was not more than ten feet, the labour of making a pier was within reasonable limits. It did not need to be built up clear of the water: in fact a pier whose top came to within an inch or two of the surface acted as a safety valve in times of flood. It was the high handsome piers which caused the banks to collapse.

A second reason for our increasing regard for the piers was the way they cleaned the mud away, leaving a clean gravel bottom for as many as twenty yards downstream. We seemed to enjoy our biggest successes on the downstream side of all our ventures, including those which originated in the bar.

Setbacks were, of course, part and parcel of the partnership, and sometimes they were serious. Once at least they were almost lethal.

There was the occasion when Joe drove me up to the quarry on a Sabbath morning and with reverent care produced an egg-like object from one pocket and with even more care a short finicky thing like a pencil on a string from the other. Years later I should have known just what to do with it, but in the ridiculous peace we were all misusing, the function and appearance of a Mills bomb were a stranger to me. And so apparently was it to Joe. He had acquired it from a territorial friend in return, so he said, for the recitation of a poem about a lady called 'Lil' Joe's idea was to blast some rock, a reasonable idea enough in view of the increasing dearth of good sized lumps remaining. As most of us have done murder with these weapons since – or at least practised it – a description of Joe's panicky jabs at the detonator in order to get it to seat inside its bomb will seem unreal. But that fair Sunday morning which culminated in a noisy explosion and the smashing of the windscreen of the car was, to us, a landmark in our labours. It didn't get us any rock – pushing Mills bombs into cracks doesn't work – and for another thing it cost us more than a trifle each in the county police court. Yes – one of our failures – although it was retrieved within a fortnight by the brother of our cook. Parochial as is this episode in the development of the burn, it had its significance. Cook's brother was a shot-firer in a coalmine, and in return for a blank cheque at Jenny's, he removed enough rock from the face of the quarry with a little something he took from a brown paper parcel to last us a lifetime. This time we took the policeman into our confidence, and in spite of the expense, it was worthwhile.

Another failure became obvious to us at about the same time. There was a place where the stream had been canalised by a bank of rushes into a narrow and sluggish channel. The rushes stood in water-logged mud, and we had set about pulling them up during the second season. We pulled them up all right – or at least some of them. But the mud remained, and the stretch began to take on the aspect of a cess. I believe that it would have been better tactics to have either filled in the bog and made it all dry land, or made the stream do the job for us by erecting hurdles and waiting until the mud built itself up into dry land.

Guests who came out to fish the burn did not always do well. A few were defeated by it and went home frustrated, and not altogether convinced that it held good fish. The fact is that it required a specialised technique which was a cross between jungle fighting and a commando raid. The fish became as wary as deer and each individual rise had to be studied as a separate problem. Most sporting fish are shy, although they react in different ways to assault. Salmon, for instance, frequently appear to take no notice of an angler, even if in their own way they are aware of the colour of his tie and have observed the maker's name on his rod. They may lie motionless and it may only be their continued persistence in refusing every kind of lure which rouses a dawning consciousness in the fisherman that he has been a clumsy lout. Trout, on the other hand, dart away into the reeds or shelter under the banks or stones at the first sign of hostilities, and I always believed that our special trout were quicker than most in this respect. The merry angler with big feet and breezy manners never stood a chance.

Consider the Willow Pool, it was best approached from the south bank which was high and slippery and gave a poor foot hold at its base. A circuitous detour through the field to a point at least thirty yards downstream was advisable, and even then it was necessary to see that your shadow in no place overtopped the bank. There is nothing so effective as a shadow for making fish scatter. Once you had lowered yourself down the clay face, the approach was begun a yard at a time, and during the last ten yards it was impossible to move too slowly.

The pool ahead was cradled in a left hand bend, the willow leaning out from the far bank in its elbow. That bank was only eighteen inches high, while on the angler's side it was now much lower and grass covered. The morning sun threw shadows upstream and the gleam of the rod fired its lightning into the pool.

By this time one knee was firmly planted in a bed of oozing mire, and you suffered this until you had seen a fish rise and decided on the right tactics. It was more than likely that your efforts would culminate in a single cast, and if this was bungled it was time to try again somewhere else. The choice of casts was limited to two. The first one was a throw of about seven yards to a patch of water under the tree itself. There was initially nothing very difficult about it, for

we had cut back the branches so that there was approximately a foot to spare between the right length and disaster among the foliage. A good fish always lived here and whenever it was on the feed it hung between the swifter current running into the pool and the quieter and deeper water under the tree. The line of demarcation was clear – as could be demonstrated any day by making a cast which was a foot too long. Then the drag on the fly had to be seen to be believed.

The second cast, and on the whole the easier of the two, was one which was made to a point on the water out of sight of the angler; upstream and round the bend. It entailed a throw which laid all but the last few feet of the cast and line on the grass and permitted the fly to swim about a yard down the channel which fed into the pool. A good fish, but not quite so good as the first, usually dined from this position. If it rose you never saw it. You only heard the splash. Quite often it was possible to make half a dozen casts without putting the fish down, for the heavier weeds had been cleared out from the inside of the bend and recovery of the line after the fly had dragged into the bank was simple. It could be lifted away with a smooth vertical stroke. It was only when the barb hooked a stubborn leaf that the proceedings were terminated.

There was an alternative attack, and this was a stomach crawl. After a little practice it was possible to get within ten feet of the bend to make a cast lying full length. It was a fair enough proposition in dry weather, and so far as I was concerned, it taught me how to make a fairly accurate throw from an awkward position, an accomplishment which years later led to the downfall of a salmon from a position within fifteen feet of its lie in gin clear shallow water.

Now these gymnastics were not difficult. They only needed patience and endurance. The difficult part of the business began when you came to place the fly accurately on the water. It was here that the wind would produce a counter attack which could convince you that the devil was in league with it. The high banks created eddies which on the back cast would make the fly behave like a glider on the lee side of a mountain, while towards the finish of the forward drive it would interfere again and try to throw the fly back towards you. Just what happened depended on the force and the direction of the wind, but it is true to assert that the air flowing eight feet above the stream was never in the same direction as the air on its surface. There were actually places on the burn where a particular wind would prevent your fly from alighting at all. An up current would hold it suspended until it tired of the game, and flung it aside on to dry land.

But, as many a saint has discovered in the past, the devil can be defeated, and his defeat on the Willow Pool could be brought about by a low sideways cast in which the fly was never more than six feet above the surface and always under the shelter of the bank. The cast had the additional advantage of laying the line up the current, while a check just before the fly landed put a couple of 'S' bends into the cast and helped compensate for the drag between the slow and the fast stream.

With reasonable luck the elbow of the pool was a fifteen minute job, and if it failed, the stream above was always open. If you took a fish under the tree and brought him downstream, the water above still remained undisturbed, and you might get a second trout afterwards. On the other hand, however large the fish, it was fatal to stand upright to play him. The water above was automatically ruined if you did.

There were other places which demanded quite different tactics, and yet in their own way called for contortions on a high level. It was really little wonder that visitors failed. Joe had a method of fishing the run above the Bath Tub from a platform kicked out of the almost vertical clay bank on the south side. Some very good fish used to lie in the neck where the water increased in depth. It was a channel formed by an artificial groin which narrowed the stream from a dozen feet to little over a yard – a barrier shaped like a 'V' with its apex left open. Any hatch of flies would swim down it in columns, to the utter contentment and convenience of a trout. The normal way of fishing it was from the lower end of the Tub with a longish cast, never very satisfactory owing to the angler being directly below his fish. The opposite bank which was low and lined by rushes would have been the obvious approach if it hadn't been for an awkward set of the current which seemed to snatch at the line as it alighted.

So Joe kicked a platform for himself in the bank. When he was in occupation he looked like a daddy-long-legs on a wall. With a line of a few yards he could cover the vital area almost regardless of the devilments of the wind, and it was that slight angle off the lie of the fish which made all the difference. He took a number of trout up to three quarters of a pound from his perch, netting them dexterously by leaning outwards over the deep water without overbalancing. It was a solution to a tricky problem until one rather cold day his platform collapsed. It was this accident which finally settled a disputed point about the depth of the Bath-Tub. Standing upright, Joe claimed that his chin was just awash. We made it, therefore, that the water was five feet, five inches deep – a really fine hole for so small a burn.

The slow bit of water below the cattle ford was another place for special tactics. It was here that we had tried to pull out the bulrushes which forced the stream into a deep, straight, but sluggish channel under the north bank – an effect which went by default, and yet left some good trout to rise there on warm evenings. It was also here that I had the worst moment I have had while fishing. I call it a moment, although it seemed like a thousand years – the misunderstanding with the Brindle Bull. The beast had crossed the ford above in company with a number of heifers and, apparently assuming that I was a rival, decided to beat me up. If the subject was less of a favourite with the funny papers, I would pen a powerful paragraph on the horrors of the situation. As it is, it is sufficient to state baldly

that after pawing the ground in the accepted style, a ton of beef came in my direction at a smart pace. There was no escape, except perhaps into the quagmire of rushes. So in Camelot-style, I held the rock like a lance as though to impale the enemy – an act born of despair and not of courage. The bluff succeeded, and the beast turned away a couple of rod lengths ahead of my lance. It went past and into a tight right-hand turn with a most unpleasant noise, and while thus occupied (a bull takes quite a time to complete a circuit at full speed), I did some riming on my own account. A second charge followed, but I won the ensuing race to a hard piece of bank from where I could take off across the water by an uncomfortable margin. For ever afterwards I carried a .32 Colt while fishing, and Joe produced a forty-five! When I complained to Charlie he roared with laughter – and it is doubtful if he believed me. Brindle Flanks was a model of sobriety in his eyes – no more aggressive than the oldest member of a gentleman's club. Charlie couldn't see that if one had, as it were, inadvertently occupied the oldest member's favourite chair, that the old dear could become a raging maniac. But it was not long afterwards that Charlie himself came round to our way of thinking. The bull caught him in the middle of one of the small fields on the far side of the big barn, and Charlie – standing his ground because he couldn't believe his eyes – found himself engaged in single combat. I have said that I saw Charlie throw the bull. It is not true – for by the time I arrived on the scene, he was sitting on its head and Jock was advancing across the field with a muck fork. The bull had had enough – and so, I think, had Charlie. It lived thereafter with a chain through the ring in its nose, and the other end of the chain was always kept anchored.

To return to the water in its channel beyond the reeds, there was one infallible method of fishing it. No ordinary cast stood a chance, for at the first throw the line was carried round the toughest bulrushes in the county. Nor was it feasible to fish from the opposite bank, for once again a crumbling cliff stood in the way. Even Joe agreed that a perch on its face was without a future. So the stone-fly creeper was enlisted, baited on a bare hook, secured by a turn of the finest tying silk, and lowered over the top of the rushes to the waiting trout. The stone-fly in this stage of its lifecycle is a nasty looking customer but of a size which places it in the category of a main course. When in due season – which, as far as I can remember, was onwards from July – it would appear on the burn in small numbers and be taken greedily. It was then that this ten yards of water came into its own.

The object of the angler was to place the creeper on the surface the right way up, and then without any part of the cast touching the water, to swim it downstream. This meant supporting the marionette on a string and following its course down by matching the swing of the rod to the speed of the current. It was exactly the same thing as clapping with a dry fly, but unlike a dry fly the trout took the creeper with a heartiness which usually ensured that it was securely hooked.

The first approach, of course, was to catch your creepers, and there are no doubt better implements than the lining of a hat, or a square of silk neckwear. Still, failing a successful grab with the bare hands, these were the poor tools which were used. To mount the creeper so that it didn't float bottom upwards – in which attitude it had fewer attractions for the trout – was another problem. The whole apparatus had to be treated with respect – swishing the rod or light hearted casting would flick it off. It is quite true that creeper fishing is an advanced form of angler's mania, for the trout in the gut never seemed to increase in weight much beyond a quarter of a pound. But it amused us – and as a method it is apt to be deadly.

The spotting of the rise was the first move. This could best be done from below. Then came the approach and a slow parting of the reeds – oh, so slow! It was better now to wait until the fish came up for a second time so as to make sure of its exact position. The dangling creeper could then be lowered inch by inch on to the surface. It should initially just 'kiss' the water, if possible not even breaking the surface. The moment is exciting for an immediate rise is the probable response. There is often the briefest of warnings, for at this close range the fish can usually be seen coring up from the depths, its jaws open. The best thing to do is to drop the rod point as the creeper disappears – an action which runs contrary to every instinct, and is very difficult for this reason. If you don't do it, however, it is more than easy to flick the creeper out of the trout's mouth and, as with a dry fly, this is the last you will see of the fish. Such is the enthusiasm for a stone-fly, however, that a delayed strike is quite safe.

Like every other raid upon the enemy, stealth of movement was of paramount importance. It was astonishing how slow our visitors were to realise this. It convinced me that nine fishers out of ten throw away their best chances on small waters. And if they only realised it, they probably ruin many another good chance on larger waters. I remember an object lesson on just this point given me by a fisherman on another river. We had gone down to fish a pool after dinner in the dusk of a summer evening. The approach was through a wood which opened out on to a bed of shingle with the pool beyond. On the other side were more trees clambering over a precipitous bank. The water flowed blue-black in the dusk in a tossing stream, perhaps twenty five yards across to the corner where the river bent in towards us – and out there two big trout were rising. There was plenty of opportunity to observe them while my companion with infinite care and deliberate slowness oiled his fly.

I thought that he was never going to be ready, and I was increasingly impatient to see his 'Coachman' put over the lower fish – for that trout was something unusual. I stayed to watch instead of going up the river and trying the pools above. It seemed as though I might enjoy a demonstration of the methods which had given my friend the reputation of a magician. I am glad that I witnessed his performance, infuriating as it was. Long after the time that I myself should either have had both fish on the bank, or put them both down, my companion was still on the edge of the river making apparently desultory casts over the near side of the run at – least eight yards short of the lowest fish. He was moving like a tortoise in low gear, and when he caught a trout of about half a pound close in to him, there was a further delay. It was only after this that with agonising slowness he moved one foot after the other out into deeper water from where he could cover the main stream. It was now that he seemed to lose his lethargic attitude.

His eyes measured the distance to the big fish, and then clearing the line with a few preliminary swishes, he cast it out and unrolled it like a stair carpet up the river. It was too dark to see where the fly alighted, but it must have been within a yard or two of where the trout had moved. When nothing happened, it seemed something of an anticlimax. So much time had already been wasted that there could be no excuse for the absence of a fast and thrilling finish. Nor was my companion in a hurry to make a second cast – apparently to the same position. He waited, and after a pause, there was a boil in the water which even the dusk couldn't hide or the rumble of the river entirely silence. The rod hooped into an arc and the fight was on. After a few breathless minutes, the fish came quietly to the net through the gentle water below. It had been worth waiting for.

I didn't wait to watch him catch the second trout (as a matter of fact he lost it after a short battle), but I had learnt my lesson. It was not merely to approach the water a yard at a time, but to tread lightly, and to fish the water nearest before reaching out to cover the further stream.

There was need, and greater need, to adapt such tactics to the burn. They have their origin in a quietude of mind unknown to many of us, but possible to acquire to our contentment and wellbeing.

The burn was mostly fished 'dry'. The truth is that most small waters lend themselves more readily to a dry than to a wet fly and such fishing is more fun than any other. To watch the sails of a Dun bobbing down a run and to see it disappear in a sudden splash is vastly stimulating. If it was necessary to catch a fish on a stubborn day, an upstream worm was, admittedly, more deadly. But we seldom used it. Worms were reserved for the churning flood waters when no other method was possible. To have consistently fished it would have cleared out the best fish in a single season.

At the same time, I admit to a warm affection for the worm, so much abused and rarely understood by the chalk stream men. It has performed miracles at moments when it was the trout and not the manner of catching it which mattered. Moreover, at its most killing time on cloudless days with a clear stream, it is no method for a ham handed fisherman. It demands the patient stalking of more educated methods, and not a little of the skill. Put a rod, a can of worms, a 4x cast, and a Stewart tackle into the hands of a novice, and let him loose on a first class little water, and as likely as not he'll come back with an empty creel. The manner of using this bait is suggested in another story.

Other lures found their way to the burn from time to time. After Joe's frogspawn had in due season produced its frogs, he had baited up a three hook tackle with one of the young. It was a bestial procedure, and I have nothing to say for it. I had less consideration for a daddy-long-legs, and no compunction at all for beetles or grasshoppers. Of these, a daddy-long-legs would never remain on the hook long enough to catch a fish, although I believe a smear of bird lime used as a glue might have accomplished the impossible. A grasshopper was more successful – after it had been put out of its troubles in a tin of crushed laurel leaves but – a beetle again was unpleasantly messy. Each of these baits was more suitable for a blow line than a burn rod, and always we returned to our homemade olives and sedges and cow dungs. They provided sport enough for any man.

One day in the early spring a familiar looking figure came over the back of the rising ground on the far side of the burn. He strode behind the plough, drawn by the two great Shire horses we knew as the Heavenly Twins – dusty greys with shanks like a pair of elephants. It was a pleasure to watch Charlie behind these beasts, not only because one could sense an understanding between the three of them, but for the sheer quality of their works.

I crossed the stream and went over the edge of the plough to meet them. We needed the services of Nellie that afternoon to fetch some more rock from the quarry. The second dam was almost complete.

It was something of a surprise on raising my hand in salute to discover that I was greeting a stranger. He had the same shock of fair hair standing up from his head like the bristles of a brush, but the face beneath it was pale and had a strange unquiet expression. Moreover, he was wearing a pair of trousers which Charlie would never have worn – a light grey pair of slacks with a fine pinstripe – and of all things, a pair of brown walking shoes beneath them. Trouser bottoms and shoes were clotted with the dark earth.

'I'm sorry,' I said. 'I mistook you for Mr Farrell.'

'Farrell's my name,' he answered, as he pulled his team to a standstill. 'I'm Charlie's brother.'

He left the plough and covered the few paces that separated us with the slow roll of Charlie's walk. But the eyes which looked into mine were a million miles apart from those which looked out of Charlie's face. They had a restless quality about them, and he was older – perhaps forty five. The wiry hair was bleaching at the temples and the lines on his pale face were deeply carved. He held out his hand and I took it. Expecting the grip of a vice, its softness came as a shock. Sensing my surprise, he withdrew it and held it palm upwards, looking at it. There were two weal's on the palm and a little blood.

'They don't look like a farmer's hands, do they?' he said. And turning half round, he looked down the furrow he'd just ploughed and said, half to himself: 'But it's not that bad. Charlie himself wouldn't beat that.'

It was a statement rather than a question. Feeling that any comment, even agreement, on my part, would be offensive, I explained why I had wanted to see Charlie and prepared to beat a retreat. There was an atmosphere about this elder brother that made me feel uneasy. He was not repelling, but by left me with the feeling that he wanted to be alone. Those hands must have been hurting him, and his feet in the thin shoes must have been most uncomfortable. There was an urgency about his attitude as though he had only a little time and a big job to do. And so, of course, he had. That field was a full sized job, with a gradient at both ends.

'Are you staying up here long,' I asked, for I knew that Charlie had no brother in these parts.

'Till tomorrow,' he said. 'I gave myself twenty four hours to plough the field.' As he said it, his lips parted into a wry smile – an attractive smile that lit up his face and suddenly made me aware of his relationship to my landlord.

I went back to my work in the stream and Charlie's brother

turned to the handles of his plough.

I didn't succeed in finding Charlie that day, but at dinner time I intercepted Jock, the handyman, carting muck from the byre. He fixed up Nellie for the afternoon, and for the time being Charlie's brother passed from my mind. It was the following weekend before I met Charlie again and was reminded of the previous week's encounter.

'That brother of yours was taking the skin off his hands,' I said.

Charlie laughed uproariously.

'That brother of mine goes to work in London – he comes back here to do what he calls rehabilitate himself.'

'What's he do?' I asked.

'Tom? He's a bit of an engineer. You ought to visit Tom if you're ever in London.'

It was several years before I visited Tom in London, and when I did it was a strange experience born of chance. But from time to time during our tenancy, we saw his huge figure, and always behind a plough. He seemed to come only at ploughing time, and he never stayed more than a day or two. Joe struck up quite a friendship with him. Once they went off together to see to Joe's car whose engine was being more capricious than usual, and the result was an oily and begrimed Tom Farrell and a car with a new lease of life.

'Funny chap that,' said Joe; 'he's an uncommon way with engines.'

One day when the burn no longer belonged to us, I was walking through a London square when for no reason I can assign, my eye caught the name on a small brass plate: 'Mr T. Farrell.'

I stopped and looked at the facade of the house. It was one of those fashionable mansions in the West End engulfed by the tide of commercial interests and taken over suite by suite by individual magnates, foreign consuls and the like. Was this our Tom Farrell? Before I quite realised what I was doing I was beyond the heavy door and being led by a discreet clerk in patent leathers up a broad flight of thickly carpeted stairs. In a moment I was standing in a waiting room which might have been a bishop's study – books, rich curtains, and brocaded chairs.

The clerk returned and ushered me across the carpeted landing and into an enormous room overlooking the square. There, in the centre of it, sitting at a carved walnut desk, was Tom Farrell. He was wearing a dark suit of West End cut, a silk shirt, and a ring with a diamond as big as a soya bean on his left hand. In his mouth was a cigar.

But the same restless eyes I had first met in the ploughed field were looking into mine, and although the face was older and the hair sadly bleached, it was the same man. Now I was there, I didn't know how to begin.

'Look here,' I said. 'I shouldn't have come up – it was a sudden idea started by something your brother said years ago –'

'What did he say?' The question was fired at me like a shot.

'He said: 'Look up Tom when you're in London' – and you know how it is.'

The huge face broke into a sudden smile and I saw Charlie again. He got up from the desk and said: 'My brother Charlie considers I'm a biological specimen in a golden cage, and of course he's right. But he's proud of me in his way – he's never forgotten that I could lift a two hundred pound sack 'With one hand – yes, by God, lift it above my head. That's more than you could do.'

'You set a high value on that sort of accomplishment?' I asked, keeping up my end of the ridiculous conversation.

Tom Farrell didn't answer, but strode to one of the big windows and stood looking out into the square across the top of a window box filled with some grassy stuff. At last he turned and said with a sort of savage aggression: 'You'll lunch with me.' He looked like a tiger with dishonourable intentions.

But for all that I lunched with him. A big car driven by a chauffeur took us to an expensive place, and with a sort of fierce resentment Tom ordered a bottle.

'You'd like to know why I asked you to lunch,' he said before we'd scarcely sat down. 'Well, I'll tell you – you come from the land I love.'

It was a queer explanation coming from a big man – big in both body and mind. It was followed by a glimpse of his character which was rather alarming.

Tom Farrell had been born and bred on the farm. The Farrell's were farming stock and undoubtedly the land was in the blood of their children as soon as they were born. Hairfield had been farmed by a Farrell for a hundred and fifty years, and before that there were Farrells farming in the county.

Piecing the story together, Tom rode Shire horses bareback at the age of five, could milk at ten, shear sheep at twelve, and plough at fourteen. The trouble with Tom had been his brains. He had apparently galloped through his classes at the village school with such graceful ease that old man Farrell was persuaded to send him to the Grammar School in the city by the sea. He lived with some cousins who were in business in the green market and came home for the holidays, apparently to forget his learning and to throw his growing physical strength into the work about the land. But the Grammar School wasn't the end of it. Tom developed a flair for mathematics that made such an impression on his headmaster that the great man had himself gone to see old Farrell to persuade him that his son could never be a farmer – and he never was – except for those flying visits on which, driven by something bigger than himself, he took the plough into his soft hands and forced his flabby body over the once familiar ways. The grassy stuff in his window box was winter wheat. He said that it wouldn't grow there.

Tom Farrell told me all this as the waiters hurried round us; he seemed to take pleasure in talking. At one moment he said without any sense of immodesty, in answer to a question of my own: 'I suppose I'm one of the world's greatest authorities on railways. If you wanted a line run through the Himalayas or across the Andes, you'd probably come to me.'

He talked of the places he'd been to and the jobs he'd done – jobs which had kept him sometimes for years away from England. It was no boasting. There was a breadth of vision in what he described and his eyes kindled at the memories.

'It's a nice world,' he said. 'I like it – and if you ever want a railway anywhere, give me a ring.'

He had risen from the table, a fresh cigar between his lips, and a moment later we had said goodbye. His expansive mood had cost him five pounds.

Some gaps in the story were filled in for me one night in the warm firelight of an old man's study. More years had gone by. It was a room which seemed to be filled with the faces of familiar friends – not my friends, but my host's. How I came to meet him is no part of this tale. But he'd spent his life in the Church, actively, vigorously, and he'd been famous on the Alpine peaks in the 90's, and somewhere back in the 80's it was said that he had won a match for England by kicking a goal from the half way line. He would sit back in his chair, his chubby face framed by his white hair, and talk excitingly of the England that was. And as he talked, a procession of famous names and great events would seem to pass through the flames of the fire.

It was natural that I should in turn tell him of the stream Joe and I had made – for he had been a great fisher, too – and of Charlie and his queer brother, Tom. He heard me out, and then nodding to a fresh flood of recollections that seemed to come into his head, he picked up my own tale and finished it.

'It was the woman who changed Tom,' he said. 'She was a good woman, too – and she chose the right man. Afterwards Tom was never quite sure of himself.'

I sat silent, waiting for him to go on. It somehow seemed natural for him to know.

'Tom and Charlie fell in love with the same girl,' he said. 'She was a little slip of a thing with fair hair and gentle ways – the daughter of the corn merchant in Arnton – that was the market town about fifteen miles further north. Tom was perhaps thirty at the time and Charlie scarcely twenty. Tom found her on his return from his first long trip abroad – Rio, I think it was – where he'd been working on some electrification scheme. Tom fell pretty hard – but Charlie married her. I'm not surprised – for Charlie had something that appealed to a woman which the elder brother hadn't got. You could see it for yourself when he smiled. Well, as I say, Charlie took her. It wasn't a case of stealing – for those two had an unusual affection for one another – stronger I think than even the heady passion which they both felt for the girl. Tom saw what was happening – and I don't think he believed it at first. He was so much greater a man than Charlie and so much older, that it seemed, perhaps, impossible that a girl should be finding that she liked Charlie better. No doubt he watched her – she and Charlie while they were together – she came to the farm, you see. Old Farrell was and alive then, and he, too, welcomed her. Then one day Tom knew what had happened. He told me all about it in a defiant, rather pathetic way. Poor Tom. That genius he had for figures stood in the way of his instincts as a Farrell.'

The old man fell silent for a moment, his chin resting on his clasped hands as he stared into the fire.

'I hope I did right – I sent him abroad again and then married Ellen and Charlie. After the harvest of the following year I had the job of burying her and her child.'

'Good heavens!' I said. 'What a tragedy.'

'Yes – a tragedy,' echoed my old host. 'You could have seen her grave in the churchyard – but I don't expect you ever went there.'

I had to admit that I hadn't. Then I sat thinking of Charlie and Tom and the woman Ellen I'd never even heard of in the years I fished there. And I remembered now the times I'd seen Charlie and Tom together. There was no bitterness between them. If there was anything, there was a queer unspoken admiration, each for the other.

'And you,' I said, 'were the Vicar?'

'I was the Vicar of Arnton.'

The burn is now a memory. One day it was a living thing entwined in the affections of two people who shared it for a mistress, and the next it was once again a gutter somewhere in the north. Maybe it has gone back to its little fish, and the dams and piers are washed away. Our contract with Charlie was forever, but we broke it, not because we tired of our love, but because the design for a living suddenly couldn't include it in its pattern. We both moved away, regrettably but inevitably in search of larger and better flesh pots. The move came in the winter, so there were no goodbyes. It was simply a case of the spring never coming round again. A short letter to Charlie was our epitaph.

But I have seen it just once since those days, and that only the other day. I saw it briefly a thousand feet below me as the hills unrolled and the miles were engulfed in the dull roar of engines. Suddenly I had thought to myself, 'The burn must be somewhere near here,' and then a glance at the map, a turn over a market town, a hop across two valleys, and suddenly I was there, circling the square tower of the grey church. The white road ran down from the moors where I had burnt up the miles that June evening so long ago, and there it plunged in among the trees which hid the humpbacked bridge. I could see the gleam of the water, and the roof of the inn with the chickens still running about the yard. I wondered where Jenny was, and if she was still serving home cured bacon and fried eggs... probably to some other fisherman. And there was the big field again! It had been ploughed up and it didn't look the same. There was a lot more ploughed, too; even the little field behind the barn – showing green with winter wheat. And as I circled I saw a tractor come through the top gate and a man get off to shut it behind him. Was it Charlie? I couldn't see at that distance... and Charlie hadn't got a tractor in my day. I flew low, but the man, who had got back into the driving seat, didn't look up. He drove on into the black mouth of the stable where the grey shire-horses used to live. I was just another aeroplane.

XIII

Fancy Free

Perhaps the wine was strong. Perhaps the air itself of that June evening was intoxicating. But whatever the reason, I said to the fishermen who were gathered on the lawn that I was prepared to catch a trout with a piece of orange peel.

I saw a look in my host's eye and realised suddenly that I had said too much. I should have to find an orange and either make good the boast or do some kind of penance – perhaps by eating the discarded peel.

We had been talking in a state of post-prandial exuberance of the lures through whose agency we caught the trout in the nearby loch. Some of us swore by one pattern, and some by another, until goaded by what I was sure was much nonsense, I made the remark about the orange peel. I think that my host was in sympathy with me, for he was a fine fisherman and had caught more trout on a greater variety of lures than I was ever likely to catch. Yet I could see that he considered so forthright a statement from one of his younger guests required the corrective of a challenge, and I found myself committed on the morrow to the enterprise.

The orange presented no difficulty, and I retired with it to a corner to devise a lure which would give me some sort of a chance. It was less difficult than it might seem, for a segment of the skin could be cut to the shape of a standard spoon, and if it would retain its shape long enough in the water, there appeared to be no reason why the trout, which had already proved themselves wide enough in their tastes, should not make a pass at it. I hoped that one of the big cannibals which inhabited the loch would be a likely victim and I designed my lure accordingly. It was mounted on a large triangle furnished with a red bead and a pair of swivels. When it was completed I felt that a tackle merchant would price it at a minimum of five shillings.

Yet even now, a share of luck seemed to be necessary. The cannibals were not to be caught everyday; sometimes they would be on the feed, and sometimes they would be definitely fasting. Moreover their normal diet was small trout about five inches long, and there was no telling how they would react to fruit. As for the other fish in the loch – half pounders with magnificent fighting qualities – they were surface feeders at this time of the year and not likely to be enticed. It was a cannibal or nothing.

When the sun had begun to warm the day and there was promise of yet another record temperature – it was a wonderful summer – I took myself and a boat to a narrow and shady channel close to where the loch flowed into the river. I had caught salmon ferox here

before, and the chance seemed to be a fair one. The bait wobbled attractively and suddenly there seemed to be every prospect of a happy outcome. It was a pleasant feeling, and when the lure was trolled a third time down the shady channel without result, I was still confident. Yet it was almost lunchtime before I had my reward, and then not before the bait had been loaded with extra lead so that it fished probably a dozen feet down. The scream of the relief no doubt about the quality and size of the victim. It was a big fish, and with all the dourness of the cannibal tribe, it soon bored downwards to the uttermost depths and refused to be shifted. On salmon tackle, I should have had the better of it in a few minutes, but a trout rod – and not even a spinning rod – was for a while incapable of making an impression. Had I been able to see the fish, I should no doubt have been able to apply an angle of strain which would have overbalanced it and made it fight. But even cannibal trout must give up in the end, and gradually it came to the surface to rush backwards and forwards and show itself for the first time close to the boat. It was a smaller specimen than I had believed – yet it was good enough to bear in triumph to the lodge. Its new tactics soon tired it, and when the ghillie decided that it would fit into the net, we soon had it out of the water. The triangle was half way down its throat, and I considered that the orange peel theory was justified.

I have had the luck to catch many fish on unorthodox lures, and when experience is added up, it almost seems as though salmon and trout are liable to take anything which moves. It is a theory which will never have much appeal for the dry-fly purist of the chalk stream. Its acceptance might too easily suggest that the matching of the ephemerides on the water is more of an academic exercise than a businesslike way of catching fish. Somewhere, of course, there must be a dividing line between objects which are taken for natural food, and others which attract through their qualities of movement, colour, and in some instances scent. An imitation of a May-fly which floats over a feeding fish is a deception and its success depends upon its acceptance as a natural insect. But a wet fly fished upstream may either be taken as a nymph or as a lure. Perhaps during the first part of its journey downstream, while it is still drifting quietly with the current, it is regarded by the fish which takes it as a familiar tit-bit. But as soon as the weight of the line begins to influence it, and it begins to move across the stream, it must presumably lose its nymph-like qualities and present itself frankly as a lure. The most active nymph has not the acceleration of a wet fly during the last part of its journey across a river – and yet this is the stage at which it is frequently seized.

Unfortunately one has only to acquire a theory about fishing to discover the urgent need to disprove it. I was fishing a loch one day and in the course of a few hours was reminded again that man's knowledge is still elementary. On a loch, the lure theory has always appeared more water-tight than on a river. No nymph ever capered through the shallows as the wet fly of an angler, and acting on these premises I have never cared greatly what patterns I used, believing that any moving object has an equal chance. Such cunning as enters into success lies, perhaps, in the angler's own powers of observation – whether the fish are lying in the shallows, on the edges of the subterranean ridges, close to the surface, or deep under the water. While a fly with, say, a green body may do better in the summer, the point has always seemed to be of less importance than its size, the places where it is fished and the manner of working it. Yet on this particular day I was failing to put anything into the creel under conditions which looked perfect. The trout were rising, the sky was overcast, the wind warm, and the ripple excellent. For three hours I tried every trick I knew until I was driven to the usually futile process of trying different patterns of flies. I had tried perhaps half a dozen when chance led me to an Invicta. The reaction was sensational. The trout came up for it as though I was fishing a stew pond. The first was in the boat within five minutes, the second and third within another five, and for the last two hours of the day I enjoyed sport with three-quarter pound trout which I shall never forget. Every fish was caught on the Invicta.

But time heals such wounds to conceit, and I was soon able to return to the mental equilibrium of the freethinker who, in spare moments, dresses his own flies without anxiety for the niceties of pattern. The occasional miracle was ascribed to providence into whose workings no one can ever look with profit. Should a dozen trout insist on an Invicta once in a thousand days, it is a matter for gratitude (if it is discovered in time) rather than an excuse for the postulation of yet another theory.

I have dressed my own lures for many years, and from the first day discovered that the fish regarded them with as much approval as any others. It was more than some of my friends conceded, and many a cocked eyebrow has expressed its wordless comment. Yet success is its own encouragement, to say nothing of being an incitement to excesses, so that ultimately I produced some contraptions which horrified even their inventor. Only the trout remained calm – and took them as occasion offered.

One Christmas day I was attracted by the decorations on the nursery tree and when no one was looking removed the tinsel whiskers which grew out of an extravagant Christmas blossom. They were thin strips of silver tape which might have been used for the body of a sea-trout fly had they not been given a spiral twist throughout their length. It was the glitter of the electric light on the spirals which attracted the eye and suggested that in the cloudy water of a swollen river their charms would be no less. So I tied a bunch of them on to the shank of a large hook and found further inspiration on my wife's dressing table in the form of a bottle of silver nail varnish. With this the shank was made to gleam almost as brightly as the metal hair above, and within a few minutes I had my first all metal trout fly.

It was several months before it accompanied me to the river on a night when the sea-trout were lying thick in the pools. I tied it on the tail of a cast and flung it like a spangled star into the well of darkness. It returned to the bank unmolested, but twinkling in the pale light as it was lifted from the water. A second and third time it went out without result, but ultimately a sea-trout took it and proved once again that piscine imagination is no less fertile than man's. The sea-trout was landed – a small one of a couple of pounds – and the lure again went forth on its errand. Unfortunately the efforts of a second fish were so hearty that the delicate silver hairs of the lure were sadly deranged. The spirals had become matted kinks, and soon began to break off until it was no longer pleasing to the eye. So it was discarded and a standard silver-blue substituted. The change went unresented, for another trout was hooked and landed, and as is usual in the fishing world, nothing proved. I subsequently made further examples of the same fly by raiding the box in which we kept the Christmas decorations, but except that the lure would attract a trout as effectively as any of the standard patterns, I didn't learn anything.

A long time afterwards I invented another sea-trout fly which, for a single night, I felt was a discovery comparable to many of the notable achievements of man's genius. It was invented between eleven o'clock and midnight on an evening when several buildings came down within a quarter of a mile of where I was working. It was a shower of feathers stirred up by the blast of an exploding bomb which so mixed the ingredients of some flies that I despaired of sorting them out, and taking what was nearest to hand, I created a fly which was christened the Silver Blitz. On a single night, it subsequently killed fish in a most convincing way – only to fall from grace in the end and be relegated to the status of all other infallible lures.

The bitterness of an Easter term at school was originally

responsible for my plunge into the fly dressing business. The weather had provided a series of anti-cyclones which schoolboys, and others who ought to know better, associate with fine warm days, but which in practice often create a series of Arctic miseries, from biting north easterlies to fog and frost. The playing fields were as hard as iron, and a hockey ball rebounding from a frozen heel mark put me into the sanatorium for a week with a fellow patient who spent his time making flies. He was so convincing as to the infallibility of his homemade creations, that I was inspired to copy him. With a bandage over one eye, I peered with the other one over the shoulder of the master, and before the end of the week had created the first of a long line of atrocities which, ever since, have sustained and encouraged me. The climax to my efforts came one day more than twenty years later when a tackle merchant, hard pressed for stock through shortage of materials, invited me to dress for him a few Blue Charms. I thought the shilling offered for each was poor pay, but vanity was not to be denied, and I entered the ranks of the professionals by dressing a dozen.

'They're beautifully tied,' was the merchant's eventual verdict: 'but if you do any more, would you mind dressing them longer and more heavily, and then give the heads a commercial finish with more varnish?'

'But they won't fish so well,' I said. 'They're heavily dressed as it is, and more varnish will only make the heads bigger than necessary.' The merchant looked at me and smiled sadly. 'I know,' he said, 'but the customers like them that way.'

There is certainly something lovely about the perfectly finished fly, and it was only the most persistent success with the scruffier specimens of my boxes that ultimately persuaded me that the commercial article was no better than my own. And upon the discovery, other disillusions followed fast. I found that the Jock Scott tied by one manufacturer was not necessarily the same as the Jock Scott created by another. One would be dressed with turkey as a base, the other with pheasant. One would sport peacock spears, and the other dyed swan of different shades, to say nothing of butts and tips of shimmering splendour which patently came from different schools. Then apart from the ingredients, the length and weight of the dressings and the shape of irons would vary as much as the weather on a spring day.

I took comfort from such professional licence and began to tie flies which were either dark or light, hairy or streamlined, concentrating only upon a wide variety of sizes for each shade. Other people's books, supported by experience, added weight to the theory that the size of a lure was more important than its dressings, and that more important still was the manner in which it was fished. Now and again, I was proved so utterly wrong that I derived a form of inverted pleasure which was adequate compensation, and as luck would have it, I occasionally caught a recalcitrant fish as well.

I remember a particular specimen which delivered a decisive blow to some hardening theories. It was a salmon lying in the neck of a pool where the water was fast and clear. I could see the fish by getting my eyes at the right angle, and every now and again it would jump to give me a better view. In theory at least, it should have taken a lightly dressed fly fished on a greased line – probably a silver blue, or a silver doctor, for the day was bright and warm and the month was May.

The first time I covered it, nothing happened. The second time with an even smaller fly – something as well suited to sea-trout as a salmon of ten or twelve pounds – the result was no better. Very soon, it was obvious that the fish knew all about my efforts, for it was within ten feet of my own bank and the heavy water was not more than three feet deep. But to keep up the pretence I tried an enormous lure which might have done well on the Tay in early spring. Again nothing happened, and this time I fished on down the pool, covering another salmon some yards below after changing 'back to the smaller lure. In the process I passed my first fish within a rod's length, and to show that it didn't resent me, it jumped as I passed.

The day being warm, and getting warmer, I returned to the head of the pool and sat on the bank where I became pleasantly conscious that while I was not to catch a salmon that day, I was nevertheless going to enjoy myself. Who in the month of May, with the warm sun browning one's face and a sparkling stream singing its cheerful song could decide otherwise ? The fact that a good fish was jumping clear of the water a score of feet away and refusing to be caught was no reason for serious resentment.

Perhaps half an hour passed, and as will happen at such times, I began to look idly through the contents of the many boxes which cluttered my fishing bag. There was no sinister intent about my search. It was sheer curiosity born of idleness on a spring day, a delving into the creations of dark nights which in the bright light of the morning mainly inspired ridicule. Ultimately a strange looking minnow found its way out of the bottom of a tin, a thing which had once been a real live minnow, but which had been gradually mummified by repeated coats of cellulose varnish. It was not a salmon lure at all, for a single light trout hook had been run through its body from its tail… a special hook with a shank more than an inch long. It's attraction, if any, lay in its lightness. It could be cast as easily as a fly, and though its tiny barb could not reasonably be expected to hold a salmon, it might if I so willed be substituted for the tail fly on the end of the cast. And thither, of course, it found its way. So it was that I got to my feet, and faced my old friend again, the minnow waving lightly in the breeze, and above it, on the bob, the original Jock Scott which had dangled there all morning.

A remarkable thing happened. As the little minnow worked its way across the stream, I saw in the tumble of clear water the dark, torpedo-like shape of the fish I had watched for so long. But this time it was making no jump. It was striking with the lightning precision of its tribe up towards the surface, towards the writhing little minnow which five minutes before had lain forgotten at the bottom of a tin box. But the salmon, now on the surface itself, charged straight past the bait – missed it as I thought – and completed its strike with the most decisive and hostile attack on the fly at the bob. The line was tight in a second, and in a wondering ecstasy I realised that I had him well and truly hooked, not on the minnow, but on one of the flies he had already so consistently refused.

The fish weighed exactly twelve pounds, and he played out his life in the shallow at the tail of the pool after as good a fight as any

I remember. He had been roused at last – not by greed or curiosity, but perhaps by resentment. In his fishy mind, he must have seen what appeared to be an insignificant minnow chasing an even more insignificant fly and said to himself in a sudden access of spite – no, you don't, if anyone is going to have it, I am! It was his undoing and another justification for the oddities which found their way into the black boxes.

It was usually the salmon and sea-trout which gave the encouragement to my inventive moments. But sometimes the brown trout would prove that they could be as appreciative. On streams and rivers, I must admit that no more conservative a race appears to exist, but in lochs it is as though their breadth of living space has given them also breadth of vision. I should not like to fish against a fellow angler with a dry fly on a good river when the fish were rising; but on a loch, whether in a flat calm or a storm, I should be willing to back my chances with any of a dozen patterns of 'terror' which a purist would class as inventions of the devil. There are places where such lures are prohibited – although there is no logic in it, places where the 'demon' and the Alexandra are categorised on a par with worms. Yet in my innocence I can only view them as moving lures, no worse than a blameless Greenwell or a respectable Butcher. The point which always seems so interesting about them is the size up to which the trout will take them. Even a two inch 'demon' will attract trout on a rough day, and if it is cast far out in a flat calm and worked back in a slow curve by the angler walking up the bank, I have known it to be the only lure which will take fish. It has made the practice of the poacher who uses salmon flies on his trout otter more understandable, and explains the success of a friend who one evening proceeded to demonstrate the same point by taking a number of trout with a Wilkinson which would have held a twenty pound salmon. But the most able demonstration which I ever saw was given me by my friend Angus, of whom I have written elsewhere. He fishes two demons at once on his loch, dancing the upper demon across the surface of the water like a dervish. The method will raise the dead. I have seen him bring fish to the surface to fling themselves on the dancing demon like salmon smolts in May. It is always the dropper which is taken. The thing is fiendish, but utterly fascinating. I have worked the miracle myself, but I shall never copy that exquisite dancing movement which Angus imparts with the tip of his rod and which, here at least, is the secret of his huge success.

Not long since I met again the boy who taught me to dress my lures. Like his pupil, he has not forgotten the art and he, too, admitted that during the years which separated us from that week in the school sanatorium, his fancy had made many unorthodox flights. We were at that moment standing in a plantation of young fir on the lower slopes of a hill, and between us was the carcase of a roe deer which had just paid the penalty for destroying some dozen of the young trees round about us. Looking down, my friend said, 'Have you ever tried roe deer fur for salmon flies?' As I shook my head he bent down and pulled out a handful of brown hairs. 'Try them,' he said, 'tie a bunch on to a bare shank and see what happens.'

I did, and in due time a salmon was killed on the fly.

That same night we sat over a fire talking. More than twenty years had gone by since the mature sportsman opposite had given me my first fly dressing lesson. But as we talked, it became plainer that our experiences had led us by their strange individual routes to the same conclusions. My friend summed them up when he said, 'I believe that salmon and trout can be as accommodating in their tastes as we used to be ourselves... do you remember that rhino skin we used to eat on Sundays... ?'

XIV

A Last Look

One lovely summer day I took a look at this land of which
I have written. I saw its rivers, lakes, hills, valleys, and
gleaming sands, from Scotland to Cornwall, from the
eastern seaboard to the western, and I neither hurried my breakfast
before I left, nor arrived late for dinner when I got home. In five
hours flying I roughly circumnavigated the island, saw once again
the waters beside which I had spent so long, revived memories, and
returned with my head full of pictures better than are to be seen in
galleries.

It seemed when I set out by road from my little Scottish house on the coast that this might be my last look. The war was over, and the days when it was commonplace for an ordinary man to fly at five miles-a-minute were numbered. The future of private flight was bound up with lesser speeds. The availability of two thousand horsepower engines which would conduct their drivers to twenty thousand feet in a few minutes and run the length of the island map and back in half a day, would not be so ready. Fast as future air travel in light aircraft at a couple of miles a minute may seem, I needed something faster to view the land between breakfast and dinner.

I had a fighter, and there were long range tests to make of its equipment. What better chance to see my inheritance as my grand children will undoubtedly see it – in one glorious movie show?

The tall lupins in the garden were standing motionless like coloured spires in the sunshine when I left. The same sun was still shining on them as I returned. In between I had flown a thousand miles. Even now, after years of flying, I am still impressed by speed. It still surprises me to see a city such as Birmingham go by as though it were a village passed in a car, or to jump across a range of mountains into a new countryside almost as though one were vaulting a five-bar gate. There is nothing tangible or even noticeable in the speed itself. The needle of the dial on the instrument panel may stand at three hundred miles or one hundred without any physical sensibility of the difference. The air inside the cockpit is still and warm, a fly may be buzzing round the windscreen. The world travels with you, and for all the senses reveal, the aircraft might be on the ground. But look out through the transparent panels, see the map of the land laid out below, and then a few minutes later take another look and see how it has changed. Then you realise what the pointer on the dial really means.

As I have said, it was a fine day... fine all over the island, which is rare in our latitudes. At nine o'clock I was at the end of the runway and a green light was winking from the control van. Reaching ahead were twelve hundred yards of black tarmac, a funereal ribbon laid over the living green of the young grass. At its end, I could just see the white fence which bounded the aerodrome, and beyond it the gently rising ground which set a curve to the horizon two miles away.

This take off was to be more complicated than the others which will follow it in their future thousands. There was more to do... too much to do for anyone who did not live with aeroplanes. In future we must have a lever to make us go fast or slow and a wheel to steer by... no more. But for me, with the winking green light urging me on, these were crowded moments.

I opened the throttle... slowly, for the unleashing of two thousand horsepower will swing an aircraft round if it is sudden. As it is, I have to press hard on the rudder pedals to hold her straight. I was doing perhaps sixty miles-an-hour before the lever could be pushed home against its stop. Now the surge was enormous, exhilarating, and I was holding the aircraft down. The white fence was leaping towards me, the tarmac itself was a blur. For a few seconds, some supernatural gift appeared to endow me – as it does all pilots – with several pairs of eyes. For before the wheels leave the runway, I have noted the engine revolutions, the boost gauge, the coolant temperature, and the airspeed indicator. As the wheels lift, my hands move inside the cockpit, automatically, as though they belonged to a clockwork doll. One finger trips the undercarriage lock and another flicks up the lever. The same hand moves to the throttle bar and pulls it back, while my eyes simultaneously see the undercarriage lights changing from green to red and the boost needle dropping back across its dial. Somehow the second pair of eyes sees the white fence flash below, and a third pair notes the engine revolutions drop as my hand pulls back the pitch lever controlling the propeller. I can feel the thud of the wheels as they sink into the belly of the aircraft and feel the wind as it tears invisibly into the cockpit. My other hand is winding over the cockpit hood to shut out the wind, and the half dozen swift revolutions of the handle bring a sudden peace. We are off.

Eleven minutes afterwards I was crossing the East Lothian coast near Dunbar. I had passed the mouth of the Tay, flown inside the Bell Rock lighthouse, and crossed the Forth over May Island. The fastest train of the day would have reached this point (I could see the railway line below) in approximately two hours and thirty minutes, but if I had made the usual change in Edinburgh, I should not have been here until three and a quarter hours after leaving. In the first eleven minutes' flying I had saved approximately three hours.

My ground speed was two hundred and forty miles an hour and my course 166 degrees true. To maintain this, the engine was throttled back inside the cruising range and it could not possibly be said that I was hurrying. The petrol was running out of the tank at the rate of perhaps one gallon a minute.

After another ten minutes the rounded back of Cheviot lay below.

There was a fence running along the north side of the mountain which I crossed at four hundred feet. It was probably the boundary fence between England and Scotland along which I had walked some years before. Away to the left I could see the Chillingham ridge on which I had crashed in a glider in 1938. It stood apart from the main mass of the Northumberland moors, a tree-clad ridge rising from the banks of a little river, and beyond it I had a glimpse of the Beadnell sands some twenty miles away. I had seen the same sands from my glider on that eventful flight, but a downdraught had snatched it away to deposit me in a heap of smashed plywood on the side of the hill. Today, downdraughts were felt only as rigid bumps, as a pothole might feel in a fast car.

A few seconds, probably not more than twenty, gave me a view of the silver running Coquet and the tiny hamlet of Alwinton. I had once believed this to be good sea-trout water, and from the views I had had on my belly of the big fish in the rocky pools, there had seemed to be justification for it. But it was never good water. Those Coquet trout were the most difficult to catch of any I have met in the whole wide land. There was only one man – an Alwinton man – who could catch them, and he didn't use a rod.

It was great fishing country below. In the last five minutes I had crossed the Tweed at Coldstream and two minor streams – the Whiteadder to the north and the Till to the south. I had fished both of them with an upstream worm. If I hadn't been on the way to. Cornwall, I should have made a circuit of the Otterburn Mill upon which I dropped from the wide empty moors to hold it for a single second in the panel of the port windscreen. The River Rede runs through here and on the last occasion I saw it I had taken a brace of trout from the still pool after making a house to house canvas for a pot of Vaseline with which to grease my line. I hadn't expected to find a calm pool like this, for it was a country of fast waters, and a greased line offered the only chance.

Thirty minutes out, the Tyne was crossed at Corbridge. On the high ground to the north, the Roman Wall traced a black line east and west, to be lost in the first of the Newcastle suburbs, and disappear along the crests to the west as far away as the eye could see. A Roman Camp had lain on the starboard side, its design as plain as the foundation plan for a modem suburb. It is extraordinary how the ruins of past civilisations continue to live when seen from the air. There is a prehistoric redoubt on the summit of a hill I know which is invisible from the ground, but is as clear as a map tracing from a thousand feet, and up in the hills there is a hollow where a hundred years ago the ground used to be cultivated. As far as the eye of the walker can see, it is now a heather covered fell. From the air the hundred-year-old furrow marks trace clear parallel lines which cannot be mistaken.

These thirty minutes had cut the train journey by five hours.

Above Corbridge, the Tyne divides into its north and south branches. I used to fish it for salmon a few miles higher up, and it was good fishing until the shipbuilding slump ended in the spurt for approaching war. It wasn't long, then, before the shipyard workers were picking up dead salmon on the slips at Hepburn and Wallsend, salmon choked to death by the poisonous effluents before they had run ten miles from the sea. Today, the salmon which passes under the bridge at Blaydon, which crosses the river to the west of the armament works, has more stamina than most. What was probably the fourth greatest salmon river in the country is dead.

I altered course a few degrees at Corbridge so as to fly down the eastern slopes of the Pennines. Even in the glistening atmosphere of this perfect day, I could sense the change in the country over which I was now flying. The immaculate purity of the air was surrendering to the breath of civilisation. It was becoming like a clouded diamond. The Durham coalfield, as far beneath the ground as I myself was above it, contributed its smoke from a thousand chimneys. The great steelworks at Consett almost created for a moment a titanic gloom. Yet Durham looked fair enough and the moors to the west spread out with rolling grandeur to the Nenthead and Wear Head pikes. I suppose that more coal is mined here than anywhere in the land, yet it is remarkable how unscarred it remains. It is only the motorist who has to pass through the pit villages who has the impression that this northern county is one to be negotiated at the highest possible speed. And it possesses trout fishing, too. There is a little water among these coalfields where the trout average a pound, and where once my mother took twenty-one weighing thirty-five pounds. Durham has been maligned.

The roofs of the bishop's palace at Auckland provided a check to my course – an unnecessary check, for even from a thousand feet I could see the estuary of the Tees on my left and the little village of Yarm upstream which used to be a great port where they built the 'Wooden Walls' of England. I was forty minutes out from Scotland when I slid into the Yorkshire plain – the great valley between the Cleveland Hills and the Pennines which in bad weather offers the airman a low lying channel through which he can make his way to the south. Here the Great North Road streaks north and south in a long straight line, one of the few stretches of road in the country which is straight enough to follow from the air. Away to the left, the bluff of Ralston Scar reared its rocky face to the sky, and it was round the corner from here, where there is a white horse cut in the hillside over the Vale of Mowbray, that I used to wait in a Sailplane for thermals which might carry me to the clouds.

I don't know these Yorkshire streams, although I have fished the Swale where, in a few places, the trout run large. But I was already entering a country where the rivers are sluggish and uninteresting, more adapted to fishermen with floats and camp stools.

York Minster lay below, fifty minutes out, and five minutes afterwards I crossed the Humber at Goole where there is a great 'S' bend in the river a – Godsend to the traveller in bad weather. One hour after taking off I was in sight of the tower of Lincoln Cathedral, and I had saved more than eight hours on the train journey.

South of the Humber, for a hundred miles to the Newmarket downs, the land spreads out as flat as a billiard table. From a height of a thousand feet, I could always see the blue blur of the hills which run south and south east down the centre of the land, and here and there were patches more blue than the rest... a fine smoke haze rising from Leeds, Nottingham, Leicester and Northampton. But to the east, save for the brief ridge of the Lincolnshire Wold, there was such a spread of quartered land and straight ditches as are to be found nowhere else. Only approaching the coast of Holland have I seen its like. From March, east of Peterborough, I looked across seventy miles of this chequerboard to the Norfolk coast.

I could see the blur of London when I climbed to three thousand feet over Newmarket, and here I turned south west for Cornwall. I was more than three hundred miles from my base, but less than a hundred minutes on the way. Still climbing, I left behind a roof of scattered cumulus, and went on up until the altimeter was reading eleven thousand feet. When I looked down, I found that I had crossed three counties and was over Oxford. But by swinging the aircraft through a circle, I revolved about myself the whole of southern England. London was a sprawling patch of dark colour which fitted comfortably into the ring of the gunfight, a dirty and rather insignificant blob in the middle distance. Beyond it, even through the London smoke, the Thames estuary with its twists and indentations was clear for as far as Southend. It was like looking at a relief map laid out on a table. Glancing from London to the Isle of Wight, little more than a quarter turn of my head, it was difficult to realise that the distance represented a motor journey of more than two hours. To jump my eyes from Isle of Wight to Beachy Head, a distance of seventy miles, was less than the breadth of one of the side panels. Then when I looked south west, I saw across the Wiltshire downs, across the Somerset plain, across the moors of South Devonshire, across the blue mirror of Lyme Bay for a hundred and fifty miles to the dark, clean line of Start Point. And west I saw the gleam of the Bristol Channel, an estuary which might have belonged to the mighty river of some great continent – an illusion soon shattered by a turn of the head which showed the opposite coast of what, after all, was obviously a small island.

There were cloud mountains set above Wales, hiding the earthy peaks, and towering ten thousand feet above them. They rose up behind Cardiff and formed a blinding white wall which hid the land. To the north, too, the scattered clouds were more closely gathered, so that I might only guess what lay below. But to the south, my eyes encompassed much of what comes into an Englishman's mind when he thinks of home. It was something more than a map which had come to life. Any fisherman would have been fascinated by this view, for within its framework lay the magic waters of rivers whose names have gone round the world... Meon, where the sea-trout which rise at night are bigger, more silvery, and better shaped

than any I have found in any other English river. It flows out into the Solent at the end of one of the runways at a base where I once served. Although from my eleven thousand foot eyrie over Oxford I could not see it, I marked the watery gully which was Southampton Water and into whose eastern entrance the Meon flows. Next to it, only a few miles away, lay a blur which I think was Southampton, and through it flows the Itchen, best loved of all chalk streams by many fishermen. It was not many miles upstream from here that I hooked a salmon on a dry fly while fishing for trout. Most famous river of all, the Test, was suggested by the rounded bay at the head of Southampton Water. I have never fished the Test… but like the River Dee, its acquaintance is a treat in store.

Further along the coast, my eyes ranged over the Beaulieu and the Lymington, and then the Avon where one evening, many years ago, I found myself putting a trout of one and a half pounds back into the river because it was below the size which anglers were allowed to kill. A little above Salisbury, in the chalk country through which the river flows, there is a famous airfield, and I had found myself the guest of the Group Captain in command. It was only on the last day of my stay that we discovered each other to be enthusiastic anglers and that for two perfect evenings we had remained in the garden while we might have been down at the river had we known each other's tastes. Time was short, and to show me the reach over which he had the right to fish, he took me up in an autogyro, and for half an hour we hung suspended on the rotors over the pools, moving from one to the other, while I was instructed in the manner of fishing them.

Ten minutes after leaving Oxford, the whole Cornish peninsula was taking shape. At its northern end, I could see Hartland Point on one side and the estuary of the Exe on the other. Plymouth was hidden behind Dartmoor and even an altitude of eleven thousand feet was insufficient to open up the waterways of the creeks. But St Austell Bay was clear enough, and in the uttermost distance there was a vague outline of land which I think was the Lizard. It was a hundred and eighty miles away. I passed over Blaydon, a dozen miles to the south of Bristol after a little more than two hours in the air. A full day's travel by any other means of transport had been saved. Looking down on the reservoir which is cradled in a fold of the Mendip Hills, I tried to recall the point where I had had one of my earliest fishing thrills. In the water below, I had caught the first big trout in my life... a three pounder which had caused my father agonies of apprehension while I played it.

During the next twenty minutes, I ran down the smooth sky road at an ever increasing speed, over Bridgwater, over the wastes of Exmoor, across the Torridge and the Tamar, until at three hundred miles an hour I swept low over the estuary of the Camel at Padstow. Three minutes later I was on the ground, climbing stiffly out of the cockpit and suddenly aware that the air was warmer.

It was summer here, summer in a way which it was rarely summer in Scotland. There was a balm in the air: it caressed the cheek and carried a scented, loving breath into the nostrils. A few minutes ago, the outside temperature had been just below freezing point, but the inside of the cockpit had been warm, smelling of oil and the strange alcoholic whiff of hydraulic fluids. The sweet breath of this clean air was irresistible. I sniffed it again and again. I tried to remember what it had been like at breakfast time in Scotland. It had been cool and pleasant, but different from this.

Two hours later I was again sitting in the cockpit, making a check of forty odd instruments. Then I was off, climbing steeply from the runway over the cliffs where the Atlantic showed its white lips in gentle curves. The tanks were full again, the new maps packed in sequence in their case. The land shrank in size as I climbed. The distance between the aerodrome control tower and the mess, which had seemed so long from the ground as I had walked it an hour before, disappeared. The aerodrome with all its buildings and runways was no more than a single blob. Suddenly I was seeing an entire county, and then a few minutes later the terms had changed again, and I was looking at southern England and the whole of Wales. This time I went on up to fifteen thousand feet where a blob of water on the windscreen would have frozen instantly. I turned on the heater, and settled down in high gear to a steady two hundred and fifty miles an hour.

I reached Wales by crossing the Bristol Channel from Ilfracombe to Swansea, and flew on over the crinkled land where the mountains looked no larger than mole hills in a dark coloured field. The clouds over Wales had dissolved. When I turned the aircraft and looked back, I could still see the foot of Cornwall, and along the south coast, in the uttermost distance, a blue blur which might have been the Isle of Wight. I myself was within twenty miles of Radnor.

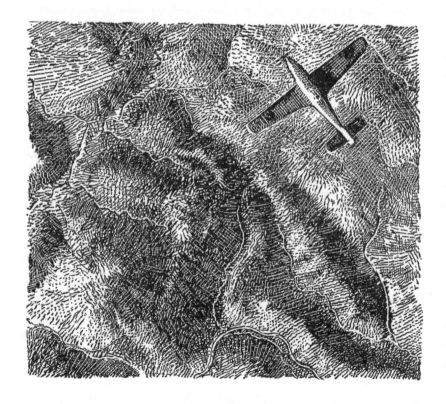

Five minutes later, and less than half an hour after leaving Cornwall, I passed over the mountain which secretes the source of the Severn, and in another five minutes had crossed the Dovey and Lake Vyrnwy. These minutes had carried me across much fishing country which I knew only by reputation. But now I was entering a land again full of memories – too many of them memories of pleasant failures. The Dovey, in many parts, is open to casual anglers and I think I may have fished it more times than most without catching a salmon. But Vyrnwy was kinder in its recollections, and so was the little lake of Tal-y-Llyn which lay half hidden under the shoulder of Cader Idris. I could see the Isle of Man across the sea on the port bow, and then close in under the belly of the aircraft the rivers of North Wales, every one of which hold salmon or trout, and sometimes both. The Conway at Bettws-y-Coed, the Dee at Llangollen where the mountains divide and pour the river into the Cheshire plain, and the Clwyd along whose banks I had been chased ignominiously by an outraged bull (for the second time in my fishing life). They are all open to a man with a rod, and if they are caught on a clearing flood, even the public reaches are worth a trial It was extraordinary how soon I was over Liverpool... less than an hour after leaving Cornwall. For once the Lancashire plain beyond was free of cloud, for once the chimneys of industrial Lancashire failed with their breath to obscure the atmosphere. The tower at Blackpool was visible for thirty miles. Morecambe Bay opened up in the north, disappearing under the lea of the Lake District mountains. And just to the north of Liverpool, I saw as a smudge on the horizon the coast of Northern Ireland, and then imnlediately afterwards the glimmer of the Solway and the Scottish coast. So it was that in a turn of the head I looked on four countries.

It was the effort of twisting round in the cockpit which reminded me that I was flying too high for comfort without the help of oxygen. I had been up here for an hour, which is long enough for anyone, unaccustomed to long flights at such a height. I remembered how I had lost consciousness in a pressure chamber and had come round again without realising what had happened – that a lack of oxygen is an insidious enemy which steals upon its victim and puts him out without him knowing it. The act of twisting my head had left me breathless ; so putting down the nose of the aircraft, I let the speed rise again, and levelled out at ten thousand feet with my eardrums pounding.

This flight was reminding me again of the insignificance of English towns. On the starboard side, the industrial belt lay crowded about the slopes of the Pennines. Great cities such as Manchester had been blobs of dark colour on the landscape – extraordinarily small blobs with vastly larger tracts of open country around them. In spite of the dense populations of the area, it was striking how much fine country still remains to build upon! I had known this before, for I had found good fishing among these cities of dreadful night. I had caught rainbow trout in the Derbyshire Wye, sea-trout in the Wyre, and among my friends have been enthusiasts for the Ribble.

At Preston, course was altered to a little west of north to take me over the cloudless sky of the Lake District. In twenty minutes after changing course, I was looking down the dark line of the Roman Wall at Carlisle from the opposite end to that over which I had flown so few hours before. The circuit of the country was nearly complete, and directly over the nose of the aircraft between the whirring blades of the propeller I could already see the pale silver of the Forth on the other side of the country sixty miles away. Again I was in a land of rivers and lochs, while far to the north west was the smudge of the islands.

One hundred minutes out of Padstow, I was directly over the top of Arthur's Seat, and had the minutes been of any real importance, I should then have rushed down the sky for my home base which I could see across the water and beyond the nose of Fife. Instead, I climbed once again, realising for the first time how much I had seen of the land today and desiring to complete the picture by looking to the furthest north. I reached seventeen thousand feet when courage failed me. Yet it was high enough to catch a brief glimpse of the north of Scotland. Not only was the southern shore of the Moray Firth standing out in hard clear outline, but the coast of Sutherland fifty miles beyond it. It was only a smudge, an outline of hills contributed by Ben Uarie and Scaraben. But beyond them I could see in my mind's eye that romantic wilderness of heather and lochs, unpeopled, uncultivated, which reached to the northern coast on the high road to Scapa Flow. I was satisfied, and throttling back the two thousand horses which had driven me so fast and so far that day, I cut downwards through the liquid smoothness of the upper air. I paid for it in a mounting pressure in my ears and, as is so often the case after flying at a high altitude, with a badly judged landing.

I was in time to say goodnight to the youngest of the family that evening. The tea things had not long since been put away and the toys still lay scattered about the lawn. When order had been restored, the long evening lay ahead of us. We decided to use it by going off on a strawberry hunt. There was a rumour that a big house a few miles away was selling its garden produce. We were lucky, and found our strawberries. While we ate them, my wife asked whether I was going fishing. I said that it was still too early, and that anyway I thought I would go to bed for a change. When we were in bed she said, 'Have you been flying today?'

'Yes,' I answered. 'I've been in Cornwall... had lunch there as a matter of fact.'

'That was nice for you,' she murmured, and a minute later she was asleep.

It didn't occur to either of us that anything unusual had happened.

IN ARCADIA

A series of beautifully illustrated books inspired
by the many faces of the British countryside.

In the Heart of the Country • H.E. Bates

The genius of H.E. Bates and C.F. Tunncliffe
combine to show the magnificence of winter
blizzards; the sudden sweet arrival of spring
blossom; the heavy scent of an August garden;
or the bronze glow of autumn light.

The Happy Countryman • H.E. Bates

Inspired by the gentle beauty of the English
landscape, the celebrated writer H.E. Bates and
the much loved wildlife artist C.F. Tunnicliffe
produced an enchanting tribute to country life.

Birds of the Hedgerow, Field and Woodland • Raphael Nelson

With a clever eye and subtle use of his
engraving tools, Nelson manages to convey the
minute differences between birds, allowing
the reader immediate recognition.